MODERN LANG

in Scotland

THE WAY AHEAD

Edited by
Alastair Duncan
and
Richard Johnstone

UNIVERSITY OF STIRLING

in association with

CILT
(Centre for Information on Language
Teaching and Research)

ACKNOWLEDGEMENTS

Grateful acknowledgement is made to the following companies and organisations which have supported the publication of this volume:

The Scottish Education Department

Bird Semple Fyfe Ireland WS, Glasgow

Caberboard Limited, Cowie

Chart Services plc, Stirling

Christian Salvesen plc, Edinburgh

Coats Viyella plc, Glasgow

General Accident Fire and Life Assurance Corporation plc, Perth

Grampian Holdings plc, Glasgow

William Grant and Sons Ltd, Glasgow

Scottish Provident, Edinburgh

The Scottish Tourist Board

The editors also wish to express their indebtedness to Barbara Macintosh who formatted and typed the text, and also printed master copies, to Ute Hitchen of CILT for her advice on many matters pertaining to the publication and to Messrs. W.M. Bett Ltd (Tillicoultry) Printers.

CONTENTS

FOREWORD

PROFESSOR A. J. FORTY
Principal
University of Stirling

This volume of papers gives a profile of modern languages in Scotland on the eve of the 1990's. Needs are analysed - needs of the individual, of commerce and industry, of the community in general; current provision is described; above all, the contributors address themselves to the future. They consider how the level of language teaching in schools can be raised, how young people can be made more aware of the importance of foreign languages, how the nature and content of language courses at all levels can be re-defined to meet society's need.

Many, but not all, of the papers collected here were given at a conference on the future of modern languages in Scotland held at the University of Stirling in November 1988. The fact that almost 250 people travelled from all over Scotland to attend the conference confirmed the very great interest and concern about the neglect of foreign languages, not only in Scotland, but in Britain as a whole. Indifference to other nations' languages has long been a British characteristic which is hard to explain, particularly in an age where travel and other forms of communication have brought us increasingly closer to other countries. Although the teaching of languages and the study of the literature and culture of other countries are largely the responsibility of schools, colleges and universities, the concern for the present state of affairs is shared by business people and politicians who are becoming increasingly aware that a united Europe is approaching fast. The removal of trade barriers and the opening up of employment opportunities within a single European community bring the question of language usage into sharp focus. The Single European Act of 1992 and the directive of the Secretary of State for Scotland that languages are to have a larger place in the school curriculum combined to make this conference especially timely.

The way ahead must be to recognise the social and economic importance of language in the new Europe, to create an awareness of the importance of the languages of other countries as a means of understanding their literature, culture, and their social and economic structures. It will require a major effort to provide teachers with the skills to meet this new challenge.

May 1989

THE WAY AHEAD

MICHAEL FORSYTH, MP
Minister for Education and Health

May I begin by congratulating you on the timing of your conference. Modern languages in Scottish education have been at a crossroads but we are now headed in a new and exciting direction. Indeed the task before us in modern languages is one of the most stimulating and formidable challenges in the new deal for education through which this Government means to equip young people for life in the 21st century.

The study of languages is of great value. Both as an educational experience in its own right, and as the key to understanding the cultural heritage of this and other nations. This has long been recognised; indeed for many years it was the study of languages which distinguished the education of our ablest pupils. Recently, more emphasis has been given, and rightly given, to the study of mathematics and the sciences but in the process language teaching has retreated to an unacceptably low level.

The task before us is not easy. There is a significant problem of attitude to be overcome. If I may quote the words of Sir Hugh Campbell-Byatt, the distinguished former diplomat and current chairman of the Centre for Information on Language Teaching and Research: "The availability and importance of English still clouds our perceptions and cushions our linguistic disadvantage."

As a major industrial nation, we simply cannot afford the luxury of assuming the rest of the world will speak English - an assumption which has led over the years to a diminishing emphasis on language teaching in schools. It would be wrong, however, to point the finger solely at education. It is an attitude which has also pervaded business and has produced a traditional overconcentration on English speaking markets.

The creation of a single European market will dramatically increase trading opportunities - there is no doubt about that. But while 1992 is a convenient and significant landmark, it is only the next staging post along a route which we have been travelling for some time.

Great opportunities exist for British firms beyond the threshold of North American and Commonwealth markets. Slowly but surely the focus of our trading effort has been shifting to Europe. In 1971 29% of our exports went to EEC countries. Fifteen years later, in 1986, that figure had risen to 48%. It is likely to grow still further. But if it is to grow as far and as fast as it should, then businesses will have to improve the linguistic competence of their employees and representatives.

This competence, moreover, needs to pervade a wide range of business activities and skills. It is not just a question of translation and secretarial services. Sales and marketing, attendance at trade fairs and international conferences, visits to suppliers, plant installation and maintenance - these are all now areas where languages have a direct part to play. And the requirement for linguistic skill is not confined to senior management and sales staff. Technical, scientific and engineering personnel are just as likely, if not more likely, to need to communicate with foreign colleagues or read foreign language, technical and research reports.

I have dwelt on the importance of languages for business. I make no apology for that because it is the area where there is a new and rapidly developing need.

Substantially less than half (about 40%) of Scottish pupils in Secondary years 3 and 4 currently study a modern foreign language. In the senior stages of secondary education the percentage drops to below 10%. But within these already worrying figures there is even more cause for anxiety. There is a marked imbalance between the sexes. Girls are much more likely to study foreign languages than boys and indeed in parts of the country only one boy in every five carries a language beyond S2. Comparisons with virtually every other country in Western Europe show this to be a dismal record. Pupils in France study a modern foreign language throughout the years of compulsory secondary education, all pupils studying for the *Baccalauréat* take a modern foreign language. In Germany, pupils studying for the *Abitur* must have taken at least two foreign languages in the course of secondary education. In the Netherlands, Scandinavia, Luxembourg and Switzerland, it has been the tradition to value foreign language study. It is to redress this unacceptable imbalance that we announced in July our new policy for modern foreign language teaching in Scottish schools. We took account of the advice given by the Scottish Central Committee for the Curriculum but, as many of you will know, wished to go further than they recommended.

The principle that a modern foreign language should be taken by all pupils in Secondary 1 and Secondary 2 is already established. We have confirmed that and we have made it clear that this study should take the form of a structured and progressive two year course.

The main thrust of our new policy affects Secondary 3 and Secondary 4. We now expect the study of at least one modern foreign language to be the norm for all pupils in those years and we shall be asking education authorities to aim to achieve this by 1992. Pupils entering Secondary 3 in that year will take at least one modern foreign language until the end of Secondary 4, normally by way of a full Standard Grade course. As you know, these courses cater for the full range of abilities and should make the learning of languages much more accessible than in the past. Curricular choice for pupils at these stages will still be wide and varied.

At the same time, we are looking to a considerable increase in pupils continuing the study of languages in Secondary 5 and Secondary 6.

Greater specialisation is, of course, appropriate at these stages and for this reason we have not set targets for additional uptake but we do expect schools to make clear to pupils the benefits of continued language study.

We would also like to see some greater diversification of languages studied. For practical reasons, French is likely to remain the first foreign language in our schools for a long time to come. But the importance of other languages, particularly those of our main European partners, have an importance that has not reflected the numbers who are currently studying them. We wish to see more pupils studying German, Italian, Spanish and Russian. Obviously, it would not be practical or cost effective for every school or even a majority of schools to maintain staff qualified to teach all these languages. There are, however, other options which we shall be asking Education Authorities to consider including the use of consortium arrangements - particularly in the upper secondary years.

We have also recognised the importance of classical languages as part of our heritage, as a valuable educative experience in itself and as one which can enhance modern language study. Opportunities for their study should continue to be available.

I would like now to turn to what I regard as one of the most exciting new developments that we have in mind. That is the introduction of foreign language teaching in primary school. We are, of course, well aware of the ill-starred experiments which took place in the late 1960's and 1970's. We know that there will be difficult problems of teacher training and teacher supply and of ensuring consistency of standards and continuity of experience with secondary schools. These problems will need to be addressed, but I believe they can be overcome and we shall be opening discussions very shortly with Education Authorities about how best we can make progress both in the short term through a series of pilot projects involving primary schools and their associated secondary school, and in the longer term by tackling the issues of teacher supply, pre-service and in-service training.

But we must not, and shall not, let these difficulties deflect us from the main purpose which is to give children the experience of learning a foreign language at a time when they are highly receptive to it. I believe this is the way in which we can lay a true foundation for a lasting improvement in language competence throughout the rest of school and beyond. It will take time, effort and resources and, no doubt, there will be setbacks. But I am convinced that this is a worthwhile and important objective and one with which we should persevere.

In aggregate, the effect of our policy will be to bring about a marked and sustained increase in the number of pupils who continue with, and are competent in, language study. We shall invite colleges of education to take this into account in their forward planning. We must ensure that an adequate supply of language teachers is maintained. We have recognised that there may be local difficulties which mean that the pace of implementation throughout the country may not be uniform, but we are prepared to work with the Education Authorities in tackling these.

November, 1988

CURRICULUM DEVELOPMENT AND CENTRAL SUPPORT

A. GIOVANAZZI, HMI

This conference is concerned with the way ahead, but in order to appreciate how we are now ready to, in fact, go ahead, it is probably worth spending a few moments showing what we have been doing hitherto.

I think it is fair to say that in no other country or educational system has there been so much coherence in the development of teaching methods and materials appropriate to the latter part of this changing century. Developments have been stimulated, harmonised, co-ordinated and supported on a national scale. They have been informed by, and have themselves influenced, the educational imperatives of the age; they have progressed systematically through each stage of secondary schooling on into the adult sector.

The advent of comprehensive education in the late 1960's widened the range of pupils who were being taught a language and saw this wider range often being taught in the same class. The Scottish Education Department was quick to identify the need to provide help for teachers in these changed circumstances and set up a project through the Central Committee for the Curriculum to support the teaching of French in the first two years of secondary school. The project engaged in an unprecedented process of consultation with language teachers up and down the country and the result was the course eventually published as *Tour de France*. It tried to give teachers what they had been asking for: materials which promoted communication as their main aim, which taught a knowledge of the country and which enabled the pupils to work in pairs and in groups at a pace and level appropriate to their individual abilities. Conscious that the prerequisite for success with the new methods and the new aims lay in the interaction between teachers and pupils, and particularly in interaction in the foreign language, the Department set up, through the University of Stirling, a research project in communicative interaction which was a detailed observation and analysis of how teachers operated in the classroom. Its value lay perhaps less in what it found out, than in the stimulus it provided for further development by focussing teachers'minds on what they were doing, and indeed, if that research were to be done today, we would find that classroom interaction and use of the foreign language were much more the norm than they were then. From that research came the *Handbook of Communicative Methodology* by Richard Johnstone, commissioned by the Scottish Education Department and distributed free to every secondary school in support of Standard Grade.

The development of the Standard Grade course in languages built upon the experience of the first two years in secondary school, and was guided, through the Joint Working Party, by wide consultation with language teachers. Encouragement and practical support from the Centre has been, to say the least, substantial. Nor did it falter during the long period of dispute. To launch Standard Grade in French, a national course was held in conjunction with an international Council of Europe language training project. Three teachers seconded nationally as development officers produced in-service training packages and a video which were distributed to all Education Authorities. Regionally seconded teachers worked on materials which were then gathered together and issued throughout the central support group to every school in the country. At the same time, nationally seconded development officers, in association with the broadcasting companies, produced analytical guides to the broadcast media in languages showing how they could be used in teaching Standard Grade. These materials were also distributed free to every school in the country. A substantial amount of support material was then produced in German and again issued to every school. Similar packages are about to emerge from the printing presses in support of Spanish, Italian and Russian. More national training courses have been held for French and for the other languages and still more are projected within this present session. The effort is enormous, the support continuous, the co-operation harmonious. The involvement of so many teachers working together is the best kind of in-service training - not so much a cascade as a capillary system.

Fundamental to the developments from Secondary 1 through Standard Grade to Secondary 4 has been the need to accommodate a number of features which have changed the landscape. First of all, the clientele is everyone - not a selected few, but the totality of the school population, hitherto in range - in future in quantity as well. Allied to that, the injunction that the assessment related to the courses had to be couched in positive terms - in other words accrediting the pupils for what they could do rather than failing them for what they could not. This then led to a reappraisal of the actual needs of the pupils and what it was reasonable to expect them to do level for level. The pass/fail concept had gone. Indeed it was a concept which was always a very dubious one in relation to language learning. Someone scores 45 and therefore does not know French; someone else scores 55 and therefore does know French. This particular *non sequitur* had been following us for generations. The lessons of group work, participation, differentiated activities and the like which had been progressing in Secondary 1 and Secondary 2 came to be legitimised in Secondary 3 and Secondary 3. To achieve this system of positive accreditation entailed defining the criteria of attainment. When you start thinking about this you inevitably have to ask what the attainment consists of, and this in turn leads on to establishing what people actually need to do with a language. The priorities are not difficult to establish. People want to be able to speak, to understand what they hear, to understand what they read. They wouldn't mind being able to write a bit, so long as there weren't too many mistakes glaring at them from the page making them look uneducated. But then, who writes very much now - apart from retired teachers in *The Scotsman*. Even the BBC have taken off *Any Answers* because nobody writes to them any more. So we took writing out of the compulsory part of the examination at Standard Grade and left it to be examined later on at the Higher stage.

One of the most crucial features, however, which had to be accommodated was the time element. The ability to use a language and to have confidence in using it is not something which is suddenly learned. Although one can learn vocabulary or elements of grammar, sometimes quite quickly, it takes time, practice and exposure to the language before what has been learned can fit into place with ease and relative accuracy. Hitherto our pupils had been given a lot of grammar and had done a lot of writing and emerged at the end of school with neither confidence nor competence in speaking and with difficulties in understanding. Harry Dresner and others have referred to their disappointment at the weak knowledge of grammar of their incoming students. But this is nothing new. Twenty years ago, in the very same department as Harry Dresner, we found exactly the same. And some years before that in first year at university two different language professors descended to the first year prose class furious at the abysmal elementary mistakes which peppered everyone's pages. And those students had been the cream of a selected cream, who had studied French (and usually Latin as well) for at least seven periods a week for five or six years. And nobody could hold a conversation. Clearly the man hours had not been expended in the most effective way. There are not the same man hours available now for language teaching in our schools, so priorities had to change. The priorities had to change in order to achieve better standards of those skills which are now most essential and also to provide a profitable, and enjoyable educational course for the pupils. Not enjoyable for the sake of attracting pupils to the subject, but enjoyable because it is axiomatic that one does best what one enjoys doing.

The reforms have been carried on into fifth and sixth year with the reform of the Higher and Certificate of Sixth Year Studies. These take forward the development of discussion skills, student responsibility and interaction in class already begun at Standard Grade, and whose absence in the upper stages of our school was highlighted in the HMI report *Teaching and Learning in the Senior Stages of the Scottish Secondary School*. Recent investigations have shown that people who claim to be able to socialise at a gentle level in a foreign language have no confidence in being able to negotiate deals and the like. This must come from a long experience of language being taught as though it were a hobby, whose only purpose is, at best, pleasant chit-chat. When something important had to be said, English was used. The revision of the Higher course in modern languages now aims at promoting real discussion among the students, pushing their linguistic enterprise beyond the safe constraints of practice phrases and everyday exchanges. To quote from the introduction to the arrangements document: "The Higher Grade course embodies a further development of those practical language skills begun in Standard Grade, but with contexts designed to set the students on the road to developing some maturity of mind". Time, of course, is again at a premium - this time not so much the number of periods within the week as the length of the course itself. Many would argue that in order to achieve this maturity of mind, our pupils need more than two terms of Secondary 5. The Department, once again, has been active in supporting the revision of Higher and CSYS, and a substantial package of support and exemplar materials with guidance on teaching methods is about to be issued free to every school, and will form the basis of a national training course to be held at the end of this month, November 1988.

These same principles and objectives form the basis of the Modern Languages Modules in the National Certificate, proposed by The Scottish Education Department in the Action Plan and taken forward by SCOTVEC. These are proving particularly attractive to adult learners, both in vocational and in leisure courses, and are also beginning to find a place in short courses in senior years in school - often known as crash courses. Here again support on a national scale has been forthcoming. Through CAST (Curriculum Advice and Support Team), the SED, with the co-operation of local education authorities, has produced a body of exemplar material and guidance for French, and is about to issue a similar package (this time including a video) for Spanish. Preparation of a similar body of material for Italian will be under way shortly. The flexibility of this type of modular provision, with its appeal to learners who do not want to undergo the psychological constraints of a single final examination, has provided a structure within which teaching can also be developed in much less commonly taught languages, and, in fact, module descriptors have already been produced in Japanese, Chinese (Cantonese) and in Urdu.

We thus have a system which runs from Secondary 1 to Secondary 6 and on into the FE and adult sector, which takes communicative competence and confidence as its first aim, which promotes differentiated objectives, which is centred on the learners' needs and aptitudes, and which is supported by a system of training and materials which help teachers to operate group and individual methods in their classes.

This account is necessarily sketchy, but I hope coherent enough to underline that very coherence that binds together all our developments. With this background, we can now have greater confidence in trying to establish language teaching in primary schools. During the late 1960's and early 1970's, there were a number of attempts to teach French in primary schools, and all of these eventually came to grief. In Scotland, many of the initiatives were taken by enthusiastic individuals, not benefiting from the support of an overall policy. In other cases even where the Education Authority had operated a controlled pilot project, the projects disintegrated when they reached secondary school, since the situation in Secondary 1 was so completely alien to the prevailing situation at Primary 7. In other cases, even where the Education Authority had provided new teaching materials for primary schools, the ultimate uptake essentially depended upon individual initiatives in the schools. Above all there was no central ministerial policy stimulus. At the same time, there was in England a much more controlled project in primary French which was subject to evaluation by a research team at NFER. Its results were published in *Primary French in the Balance* (Clare Burstall, NFER 1974), and its final conclusion "tipped the scales against a possible expansion of the teaching of French in primary schools". When one reads the reports carefully, however, fourteen years later, it becomes clear that the primary project was premature, that it was placed in a pedagogical environment which was inimical to its success and to its expansion upwards into the early years of secondary school. NFER found that many children were discouraged and suffered failure, wanting to drop French as soon as possible. They identified the problem as essentially one of methodology, since the methods of the time assumed every child progressing at the same rate. "Unless there is a sustained effort to redefine the objectives of teaching French in order to meet pupils' differing needs, some children will not realise their full potential, while others will inevitably experience failure." What I have been showing this afternoon is that since then the curricular developments which we have engaged in in Scotland have in fact led to the objectives being redefined in terms of communication and to differentiation of needs being built into the methods now in use and being reflected in the assessment at Standard Grade. Furthermore, NFER also found that secondary schools accentuated the failure of some children by refusing to establish mixed ability classes in First year, and by insisting on streaming straight away. Circumstances in Scotland today are very far from that picture. There was also the objection that teaching French at primary school increased the dominance of French in secondary schools at the expense of other languages. This would still be a danger if we were to consider only French, but policy on diversified language provision is now much more positive and we should be able to diversify primary language projects as well.

The pedagogical climate has altered, the insights and methods of teachers in the early years of secondary schools are much more in harmony with those of the teachers at the upper stages of primary schools. We hope to establish a prudent series of projects, in different languages, in consultation and collaboration with Education Authorities. We are confident of being able to make steady progress so long as we are able to work within a controlled plan and are not subject to evanescent enthusiasms. I have said more than once that time is the essential factor if a language is to be acquired to any degree of fluency and ease. The theme of this conference is that we need our future generations to be at ease in other languages, to be at ease with other people and other mentalities. We can now give them more insights at an earlier age and more time to be comfortable in another language.

Each sector of education has been adapting its methods and approaches to meet the needs of the future. Just as the early secondary years are now more in harmony with the upper primary, so there are hopeful signs that the upper secondary and higher education and university may be dissolving some of the ice that has sometimes kept them trapped in their separate Alaskas. Language teaching itself has often been trapped in its own self-sufficiency. If language is a tool, then it needs to work on real materials, and that means real subject matter. In other words, the contexts which are used for language learning must be drawn more and more from the areas of the students' other studies. For our aim is not so much to produce more linguists as to ensure that most people, whatever their occupation, are linguistically comfortable, and confident that they can use their language for real in their own reality. That is the challenge. We have the structures, we have the back-up, and now we have the will.

November 1988

THE FUTURE PROVISION OF MODERN LANGUAGES IN STRATHCLYDE REGION

FRANK PIGNATELLI
Director of Education
Strathclyde Region

In line with its policy of support for multicultural education, Strathclyde region has consistently promoted the learning and teaching of languages in its 188 secondary schools which cater for about half the population of Scotland. For example, steps have been taken to provide significant curricular and staff development support for the implementation of Standard Grade courses in French, German, Italian, Russian and Spanish; support has also been made available for the establishment of school exchanges through the Strathclyde International Exchanges Unit and through grants for school exchanges and support for preparatory visits by teachers.

In its response to the SED consultative document "Curriculum and Assessment in Scottish Schools: A Policy for the 90's", the education committee confirmed expressions of regret that languages other than English had been omitted from the core curriculum for Secondary 3 and Secondary 4 pupils set out in the Consultative Committee on the Curriculum's national guidelines for secondary schools. The authority noted that such an omission left Scotland in a unique position in Western Europe in respect of the place of modern European foreign languages in the curriculum for pupils up to the statutory leaving age.

The region welcomes in general terms, therefore, the change in policy announced by the Secretary of State for Scotland and described in SED Circular No. 1178.

Implementation of SED Circular No. 1178

A regional working party has been established to make recommendations on a phased implementation of the circular. Membership comprises head teachers, members of the advisory service and representatives from colleges of education, under the chairmanship of an education officer. Two advisers in modern languages have been given additional support for their divisional work to enable them to devote most of their time to the work involved. The working party has identified four main areas for consideration:

1. The inclusion of a modern foreign European language in the core curriculum of all pupils from Secondary 1 to Secondary 4.

A major survey has been undertaken in all secondary schools to establish the current provision of modern languages and present staffing levels and qualifications. A questionnaire has been issued to all modern languages teachers in post - about 800 including part time staff - and to all teachers who have applied for a post in the region's schools in order to establish training needs, both in refresher courses in methodology for returning teachers and in refresher language courses in languages other than French for both groups. About 80% of Strathclyde's modern languages teachers are qualified to teach two languages: 48% in French and German, 17% in French and Spanish, 11% in French and Italian, 2% in French and Russian.

Recommendations will be made on a three-year phasing leading towards the inclusion of a modern language for all pupils in Secondary 3 by 1992, with projections of additional staffing requirements and estimates of training needs, both initial and in-service. The Region estimates that 200 full-time equivalent teachers will be required to implement the policy of a modern language for all pupils in Secondary 3 by 1992. This figure of 200 teachers makes no allowance for natural wastage. The largest intake of new teachers will be required in 1992-93.

2. The need to increase the number of pupils learning languages other than French.

It is considered unlikely that the desired increase can be achieved by an increase in the number of pupils studying a foreign language in Secondary 3 and Secondary 4, traditionally the most common means of providing for the learning of languages other than French. The working party is likely, therefore, to make recommendations on the desirability of seeing a significant increase in the number of schools offering a diversified provision in Secondary 1. At present, 25 schools in the Region offer two languages in Secondary 1: four of these offer French and Spanish, the remainder French and German. The need to provide a coherent policy on the provision of *ab initio* courses in Secondary 5 and Secondary 6 will also be examined. Recommendations on the provision of classical languages will also be made by the working party.

3. The provision of modern languages in the primary school.

It has been decided to establish ten pilot schemes in the teaching of French and German in primary schools from October 1989 to complement the six national pilot schemes recently announced by the SED. Ten secondary schools and their fifty associated primary schools will be involved. This first phase of the project will be limited to the last year of primary education, Primary 7. In session 1990-91, the pilot schemes will be extended into Primary 6, and new projects will be added in Italian and Spanish. In line with regional, social and economic regeneration policies, these projects will be based in all divisions in Strathclyde and will give experience of this exiting development to pupils in a full cross-section of schools including those serving areas of multiple deprivation. A major commitment in the provision of curricular and staff development has been made to these projects. An important feature of them is that the foreign language will not be taught in isolation, but will be related in various ways to aspects of the primary curriculum, for example environmental studies, the expressive arts and language arts. The visiting secondary teachers will thus work in close cooperation with the primary class teachers, who will undergo in-service training in the form of brief intensive courses in language familiarisation.

4. The provision of Gaelic and Asian languages.

Recommendation will be made on staffing, curriculum development, syllabus, certification and timetabling implications for Gaelic and Asian languages in the light of Circular 1178. The Region is aware of the cultural importance of these languages for the community. It intends to build on the support already given to Gaelic units in primary and secondary schools.

Conclusion

Strathclyde Region is aware of the exciting challenge ahead in making such radical changes in the provision of modern languages. We are convinced that such changes are essential if Scotland is to play a full role in the economic, political, cultural and social life of Europe in the 1990's. The need for support, advice and information at all levels of the education service will be crucial. Modern languages teachers have no need to be persuaded of the benefits that such a change in direction will bring: head teachers, guidance staff, school boards, parents and pupils all need to be persuaded that such changes are not only desirable but achievable. The education department is committed to working in partnership with all groups in ensuring that the challenges of 1992 are met.

May 1989

LANGUAGES IN SCHOOLS

ANN CARNACHAN
Adviser in Modern Language
Central Region

This is going to be a rather different talk from the one which I thought I would be giving when I was first asked to contribute to the conference. I no longer find myself justifying and defending the place of foreign languages in the curriculum. That has now been accepted and, with my colleagues, I warmly welcome the Secretary of State's policy statement concerning languages other than English. I should like to concentrate on outlining the educational scene today and how modern languages teachers are working to meet the needs of all the young learners in our schools and are facing up to the challenge of the policy statement and of 1992.

Aims

Firstly let us consider the prime aims of foreign language teaching - aims which are embodied in the Standard Grade developments but which influence the teaching and learning in first and second year and stretch beyond to the thinking which has shaped the Revised Higher Grade in Modern Languages. These aims are:
-    to develop communicative competence. This means the promotion of real language in real use: communication in its widest sense, enabling the learner to speak, listen, read and write in real-life situations. Speaking, however is of prime importance and this is reflected in the fact that this skill is given 50% of the weighting in the assessment scheme in Standard Grade.
- to develop pupil confidence in what they can do. It is vital to create an atmosphere of trust within the classroom where pupils will be willing to take risks with the language they are learning and will want to interact with the teacher, their peers and eventually with native speakers. This can be done in part by building on what the pupils can do rather than by highlighting errors and weaknesses. This stress on positive achievement began some time ago with the arrival of new courses such as *Tour de France* and with the thinking which lay behind their creation. For the first time, it was suggested that teachers should discuss the learning objectives with their pupils, that they should be encouraged to monitor their own performance through self and peer assessment. At the same time, the Graded Objectives Schemes, of which the Lothian GLAFLL scheme (Graded Levels of Achievement in Foreign Language Learning) is an excellent example, were setting short-term targets which pupils could attempt when they were ready, targets which were attainable with some

effort. The result was greatly increased confidence and a sense of achievement. Such revolutionary ideas are now common practice and much of this thinking has influenced the form of Standard Grade assessment in Modern Languages.

- to develop some level of awareness about language and communication. This does not mean talking about language in a dull, meaningless way but involving pupils in discovering how language works, encouraging them to speculate and to draw conclusions. This is an area in which foreign-language and mother-tongue teachers could profitably work together to provide a coherent language education for all pupils. In the future it is hoped that this cooperation can begin in the primary school as the Secretary of State wishes to investigate the possibility of introducing foreign language teaching into the primary sector.

- to develop some level of cultural awareness. As foreign language teachers, we are ideally placed to broaden horizons, to share our enthusiasms for things different and to counter the many stereotyped ideas which our pupils have. All of which means that we have an important role to play in multicultural/anti-racist education by encouraging positive attitudes to foreign language learning and to speakers of foreign languages: by helping our pupils to be open to other ways of looking at the world

- to develop social skills. If the name of the game is communication, then pupils must have the desire and confidence to interact with others. This may be expressing their own meanings in the classroom as they share interests, opinions and feelings, or as they organise and participate in learning activities. They must also be prepared to use the foreign language outside the classroom on visits abroad, meeting foreign visitors in the local community or exchanging letters or cassettes.

- to offer a sense of achievement and intellectual stimulation. I have mentioned already the sense of achievement arising from the setting of attainable targets and from stressing the positive. It is also important to challenge all pupils: to try to ensure that all pupils achieve their full potential. Certainly Standard Grade affords the opportunity to stretch all pupils: they will all find the course challenging but for the first time all pupils will have access to assessment and certification at an appropriate level and for the most able the standard required will be considerably above the present "O" Grade.

Learning

All recent reports on teaching and learning have been concerned to discuss not only what should be learned but how the pupils should learn. There is fairly general agreement about a number of permeating factors which should shape and influence the learning experiences of our pupils.

These factors are:
- co-operative learning: learning together to some end or outcome
- independent learning: to take responsibility for one's own learning
- problem solving: investigating topics and issues to propose solutions to problems
- rational/critical thinking
- finding out information: developing access skills
- using language actively as a tool for processing information and developing understanding
- trying various strategies for learning: learning to learn
- interacting with others: social learning

Most of these elements are self-explanatory but I should like to say a little more on the subject of learning how to learn. It is our aim in foreign language teaching to help our pupils to achieve an appropriate level of competence in a foreign language. We cannot produce linguists at the age of sixteen any more than our colleagues can produce scientists or any other specialists. We should be providing them with tools and strategies to help them to learn - either to continue their study of the first foreign language or to take up another language at school or later in life.

Which languages?

This brings me to the question of which language should be the first foreign language. The development of study skills and learning strategies can be achieved through any language and there is no reason why French should hold sway. I certainly welcome the encouragement to local authorities to increase the opportunities for the study of other languages. Many schools are already seeking to broaden the base of language provision and are experimenting in various ways:
- by offering two languages in first and second year, which means that 50% of the cohort do French and 50% do German or any other language
- by offering two languages in alternating years: French is offered in year one, Spanish in year two and French again in year three and so on.

Perhaps most exciting are the opportunities provided by the new SCOTVEC National Certificate Modules for students in S5 and S6 and for adults in schools. The Modules offer beginners' courses in an ever-increasing range of languages. Modules 3 and 4 can be an alternative to the SCE Higher Grade for students wishing to continue the study of a foreign language after the age of sixteen. At this level the Modular provision allows a far greater degree of vocational specialism for those who wish it.

Many young people are picking up a language again in S5 or are embarking on a second and even a third language, such as Spanish, Italian, Russian, even Japanese. Such a widening of provision has, of course, serious staffing and planning implications for local authorities. But there is also the question of the teacher's oral competence in what is possibly a second language and the fact that traditionally there have probably been fewer occasions to use the language. There is an urgent need to support exchanges and study visits to enable teachers to go abroad and refresh their linguistic skills.

TVEI and the world of work

As I have said, the prime aim in foreign language teaching is the promotion of real language in real use: the emphasis must be on developing language skills which are useful and relevant. They must be relevant to the young people, to their needs and interests, but also relevant to the world beyond the classroom, to the world of work. This brings me to the exciting involvement of languages in the Technical and Vocational Education Initiative (TVEI). Most regions are still running their pilot projects but a few have already moved to the extension of the TVEI approach to all pupils and across the whole curriculum. Each project is different but a few examples may show how our involvement is affecting the learning experience in modern languages.

The microcomputer can be a very useful learning aid in the language classroom, from the language games which can help to consolidate the learning of grammatical structures, to group participation in interactive simulation programmes. Of course, the use of the computer as a word-processor allows pupils to draft and re-draft pieces of writing and to create text on screen which can then be sent to other schools in the Region or elsewhere in Scotland or abroad using electronic mail. Interesting computer links are being set up in this way. Schools are also increasingly being able to access the French viewdata system, Teletel. This provides a constant source of authentic materials for the classroom teacher and interesting, attractive, up-to-the-minute resources for pupils. An even more immediate and attractive resource which is set to expand is satellite television. There has been some experimentation in the creation of support materials but more work has still to be done. Ideally, one would want easy access to satellite programmes for senior pupils and college students to encourage independent viewing and supported self-study.

Students have to be able to communicate in the foreign country but should also be able to cope with foreign visitors in the local community. In our teaching programme, it is important to build in activities which highlight the needs of the local area for language skills. TVEI requires all pupils to have a work experience in S4 and wherever possible there is an attempt to place language students in a firm where they will be aware of the impact of Europe, where they may be called upon to deal with foreign correspondence or a telephone call from abroad. In the light of this, some language departments are collaborating with Business Studies departments to deliver training in understanding and writing business letters in a foreign language, dealing with the telephone etc. For pupils after the age of sixteen, there have been a few experiments offering students placements abroad where they can work-shadow or study a particular aspect of business practice. This is an area ripe for development particulary in view of recent Council of Europe initiatives.

TVEI also seeks to promote a student-centred problem-solving approach to learning and to develop learning experiences which encourage the personal and social development of each pupil. That brings us full circle to the kind of learning which I described earlier. Learning which I believe young peole will find more challenging, more relevant and more enjoyable. Certainly this is beginning to be seen in pupils who are now going through Standard Grade and I would hope that this positive experience will encourage more students to continue their study of languages. However, they must be made aware of the advantages in doing so, aware of the many courses and combinations now on offer in Higher Education, aware of initiatives like ERASMUS, aware of employers' need for a work force competent, to varying degrees, in the languages of present and future trading partners.

Conclusion

I would not wish to pretend that everything which I have mentioned is happening in every school, but the momentum is growing through Standard Grade, the Revised Higher, SCOTVEC Modules and TVEI. What has been described is happening across the country to a greater or lesser extent. But we are talking about radical changes.   Future support for staff must include staffing levels to do the job well, resources, opportunities for staff development and for study visits abroad. This is an exciting time in the development of foreign-language teaching. Teachers in Scotland are moving forward to meet the challenge of the way ahead.

November 1988

LANGUAGES IN A CENTRAL INSTITUTION

HARRY DRESNER
Head of the Department of Languages
Napier Polytechnic

Central Institutions are not a very homogeneous group; the only two much alike as far as languages are concerned are Napier and Glasgow College. Similar levels of language work are more likely to be found in major FE Colleges such as Aberdeen and Dundee Colleges of Commerce than across the range of Central Institutions themselves. It has been agreed therefore that what I say today reflects what is happening in one Central Institution, now called for its sins, Napier Polytechnic of Edinburgh, but I trust the issues raised will have a wider application for courses in business and in science or the technologies elsewhere.

"Young people who believe that a foreign language is a vocational qualification are the despair of careers officers. On its own, a language is next to useless". Such are the opening lines printed under LINGUIST in the Sunday Times Good Careers Guide. The Guide reflects the traditional attitudes of employers in Britain, though not in Europe at large, when it goes on to say that language skills must be regarded only as a bonus; for example in export sales, and even the diplomatic service.

In my own institution we have never tried to run a full-time languages course as such. The full-time courses we have devised both inside and outside the Languages Department have all been interdisciplinary and mainly business-oriented; also, strictly speaking, not languages-led. We have added languages, for example, to European Marketing or Business Studies or Commerce and have had to make our language syllabuses reflect the content of those subjects. So they have become generally rather utilitarian, teaching correspondence, translation, business interpreting, business situations, social, political, economic structures and themes, and the like.

Most of the staff in languages have some exporting or other business experience or qualifications and have actually come to identify to a fair extent with business and commerce themselves; though they do still harbour some cultural and literary hankerings and pretensions.

Imagine the mixture of delight and offence we experienced when we received the following outspoken reference some time ago for an applicant to one of our courses, written by a university tutor who shall be nameless. It goes something like this.

"X finds the university course in languages excessively literary. I suspect he considers the Faculty of Arts to be an Ivory Tower and would like to take a languages course in the Real World, combined with business studies or marketing. He is a Philistine who will be at home in the world of business and commerce."

As former Arts graduates ourselves we found its withering contempt refreshing. The courses in our sector are indeed strictly "applied courses". The cultural or literary heritage that goes with the language has perforce been jettisoned.

However, I think that the examinations and syllabuses of both our CNAA and SCOTVEC courses do match the needs of industry and society quite well, if not some of the educational needs of the individual. There are, of course, still a lot of Humanities-based language courses in English Polytechnics and the colleges which remain unbalanced in the opposite direction.

The present government's initiative to launch Language-Export Centres throughout the UK to teach languages to executives and others in industry and thereby boost exports is being actively pursued in Scotland. The Language-Export consortium of Scottish universities and colleges has recently achieved official recognition and PICKUP "starter" funding. My own institution has recently set up a Language Services Unit with an experienced teacher as Manager to tout for work. All members of the consortium are required to make the activity totally self-financing within a few years. Let us hope it will be a successful venture and find enough customers with persistence and time, prepared to pay cost-effective prices.

As to the range of languages, we have found in the past that the only really marketable languages to include regularly in our full-time courses have been French, German, Spanish and Italian. We do teach other languages intermittently, such as Dutch, Swedish or Russian and we have concrete plans to extend the range to Japanese and Arabic. But all attempts are limited by the constraints, with a capital C, that we operate under and which are particularly burdensome on interdisciplinary courses that include languages, where total hourage across disciplines is necessarily higher and each teaching hour therefore counts as proportionally less in terms of teaching credit.

The most famous constraint is in fact that dreaded abbreviation, the SSR or Student-Staff Ratio. If you are teaching an art as in self-contained courses such as Drama, Design or Photography, your discipline is allowed a notional SSR of 9 or 10 to 1; that is an average of 9 or 10 students in front of 1 member of staff. That sounds civilised and reasonable. One can take the view that Languages for effective use in business are in a way performing arts, but ones which rely less on vision and instinct and more on a rigorous academic programme to achieve wide comprehension and accurate manipulation of forms; and then require the fairly rapid exercise of interactive skills.

According to the NAB guidelines adopted recently by SED, you should be able to teach that knowledge and practise those interactive skills with an SSR of 12 to 1, for any foreign language. That in effect will mean that on interdisciplinary courses you need to teach in excess of 20 students in the majority of your classes in languages and top 30 in some to balance specialised tutorials where you may be limited by course rules and aims to less than 10 or to even 1 or 2 people in some instances. Or by availability of qualified students; the fact that we cannot now find around 20 people with, say, either Higher Spanish or Italian, even across business courses, is perhaps not realised. They are not being produced in the schools in sufficient numbers. They have to be joined to an equal number with "O" Grade in the language to make a viable grouping and that means teaching less effectively at both levels. Some Postgraduate tutorials do indeed involve a 2 to 1 ratio for, say, individual projects for the Spanish export market and make hay of the departmental average. And the Languages Department may be teaching 5 or more separate languages and some at different entry levels, thereby forced to fractionate intakes, where other departments are teaching only one subject at one level for each intake.

There is now strong sympathy for our predicament, but it has been suggested to me, and not entirely in jest, that these groups should all just study together - "after all, we have language laboratories, don't we?" Indeed, "hyped up" claims for laboratories and those of the PILL course type of press advertisments have a lot to answer for.

My colleagues in languages used to say to me: "Don't take the SSR seriously". Now that several staff leaving over the past few years have not been replaced, however, and groupings get larger, they regard it as more than just a piece of dotty bureaucracy. Yet, as an Edinburgh institution, we have very healthy intakes compared with most colleges. I am therefore making a plea here, as I have in my own college, that if 1992 and all the seriousness about languages is itself to be taken seriously, languages must as of now be regarded as a special case in terms of student staff ratios, or in the end most languages will be driven by the ratio and their own rigour out of existence by easier subjects. Their rigour will in fact lead to *rigor mortis*. Even German has problems with student numbers and is being avoided as a study option by students with experience of it because it is considered too difficult; and yet German is a language in very high demand in trade and industry.

On the theme of practical project work involving languages, we have found that language graduates on the Postgraduate Diploma in European Marketing and Languages drawn from traditional university courses can be transformed into marketable export sales staff. It is the Project element which makes all the difference, each of the students trying to market the goods or services of a different Scottish firm. It culminates in a short market visit to Europe subsidised by firms, the students producing not only a market report but often initial orders.

The project work is especially unprofitable in terms of SSR; yet the project is the most useful talking point when students go for job interviews. As a way of finding suitable employment for graduate linguists it has proved very successful over 'teens of years, even though now the vast majority of the approximately 30 students are women. The same kind of teaching should be used on other courses, but it is too labour-intensive to introduce.

Another post-graduate group on a conversion course are all women, namely Graduate Secretaries studying languages. They can achieve higher rates of pay now, particularly in London and the South East, and with word-processing skills to boot they have little difficulty in finding employment. Yet because of the quota of bursaries available to them the numbers recruited have fallen drastically.

Women, we find, and I imagine others find it too, account now for approaching 80% of our students on business language options on degree and diploma courses. That in itself is unnatural, considering that the business community outwith the secretarial sphere is still very predominantly male. Maybe it is a case of early diligence enabling girls to shine and survive in the languages at school. Maybe that is one reason why the employment record of our HND Business Studies with Languages students, according or our Careers Service, is usually better than for similar students without languages; although it is not easy at 20 or less to get a first job with languages because there are comparatively far fewer of them specifically advertised by employers.

At that age, those combining secretarial skills with languages are the ones who most easily acquire first jobs. Of these HND students, in our last outputs, 33% are using their languages in their first jobs, rising to over 50% after one year out of college. The most common outlets, expectedly, are companies involved in the export trade.

The provision of physical resources for languages accumulated over 'teens of years is in my experience relatively good. As regards language teaching facilities we are still firm believers at Napier in language laboratories, the use of audio-lingual courses and other recorded materials. We have five laboratories, and students spend a fair proportion of their hours in them, though it is not desirable to use the headphones for more than about 30 minutes in any one hour.

There are also tape library facilities on two of our three main sites, though because of staffing and teaching room constraints, these are now available only for limited hours each week. There is a good library provision of trade periodicals and of newspapers too, and good photocopying facilities in the department. A telex machine allows rapid contact for project work with firms at home and abroad and both students and staff have ready access to word-processors for project work and preparation of materials.

We have recently installed a satellite dish, so that the use of news and other broadcasts can be pursued much more than previously, when staff relied on Téléjournal broadcasts. Students can have the opportunity to study news videos outside class in Conversation booths now, on small portable Sony Video 8's, instead of solely sound recordings on cassette. The booths are also timetabled for individual situation or conversation practice with Conversation Assistants, a very necessary adjunct to classes for examination purposes.

Both CNAA and SCOTVEC syllabuses try to divide the languages curriculum into around 50% speech and comprehension and 50% written skills. Almost a decade ago the BOTB and the BETRO Trust surveyed which skills were most in demand from British employers, emphasising speech and its comprehension most. Yet since most things in business have to be confirmed in writing and most European customers expect correspondence in their own language, that too has to be accurate and comprehensible. Lecturers have found in recent years that even most students with a Higher in the language have insufficient knowledge of grammar and syntax and that is causing difficulties on advanced courses by requiring a great deal of extra time for revision and further study. The teaching, setting and marking of written work, particularly correspondence, essay and *précis* work in the foreign language, is still a very heavy user of staff and student time.

The vast majority of our students to date are on these business-linked courses. This year SCOTVEC has allowed individual colleges to put forward more flexible course structures, for example in one course allowing students to switch out of languages after one year into something easier. Three to four hours of total time per week is sometimes inadequate to satisfy all the specialised learning goals, less than students had at school in fact.

In the science and technology disciplines there are not even that number of hours available. And yet it is in these areas that there may be a substantial increase in demand for language-qualified graduates and diplomates. Engineering and science departments feel they cannot afford to give much time away to languages, their main course having been planned to run without them for many years at maximum hourage. Some course boards, therefore, think one hour per week will do, or just a short course.

French, however, has made a good start over the past seven years because the Scottish system produces some science and technology students with "H" Grade as well as "O" Grade French. With dedicated, mainly French native speakers, and some of the science and engineering staff, we have managed to adapt classes to students' needs. Some use has been made of the *Fondamentalement* course developed in France and the staff involved have attended courses at Montpellier to learn how to exploit its starting materials for groups drawn from a mixture of disciplines. And staff believe, very arguably, that a major need for engineers and scientists is also to acquire general and business French.

A number of courses have their classes during the day because they can produce numbers which are almost half-decent, say 10 to 12 or more in a class, e.g. Science or Technology with Industrial Studies or Energy Engineering degree courses. But other courses, for example Biology, Chemistry, Electrical Engineering, and students in second and subsequent years of courses have to be brought together outside the day timetables in twilight classes. Some of these students have recently successfully taken the examinations of the Paris Chamber of Commerce for scientists and technologists.

However, whereas French has made an impact in this sphere, with German it is quite a different story. So few students come forward with even an "O" Grade that twilight classes or other demotivating unsocial hours are the only prospect, built up across disciplines. German is taught "from scratch" in day classes to Publishing and Printing diploma students and has proved useful to several when going for jobs. But it was excluded from the new degree course which enrolled this session. Similarly, basic Italian or French were taught to diploma students of Interior Design and of Photography, but were excluded from the degree structures which replaced the diplomas. The motivations for this appear very much to stem from the need to keep the teaching points for a course within the parent department and restrict total hours rather than to meet the wider educational requirement. The expressions of regret which were used at the time by those responsible for the change were very moving, though reminiscent of the walrus and the carpenter. And the gap between action and words still could not be greater as departments now vie in public to pay homage to 1992.

Still, many of the science and technology students and their tutors are genuinely anxious for industrial placements in Europe with an eye to enhancing career prospects in 1992. But to convince them of the real need for the hours of prior language study on their courses, I believe they need a sign from above. Several years ago SED made special recommendations about the provision of computer-literacy for all students on courses in Higher Education, and as a result most courses now have compulsory modules in data-processing. A similar unequivocal sign is needed now, not to make language study compulsory but to provide full language options integral to course structures and earning realistic study credits. Nothing less, in my opinion, will motivate most course boards and students to go for more than just the voluntary attendance which is prevalent now.

The Secretary of State's decision to make continued study of languages in schools more widely available will have an effect on us in five or so years time by increasing the number of students with previous knowledge.

But rewards and encouragements need to be developed now to increase the number of hours of study in our sector too.

To be realistic about language study, provision must also be made for students to have some residence abroad. Many of ours try to get casual employment abroad or a proper work placement or both, but unless residence abroad is an integral part of their course there is currently no prospect of SED funding for it, merely encouragements to use ERASMUS and COMETT. However, even the rules of Erasmus applications appear to have been re-written by a Renaissance genius, so narrow is their actual final relevance to the majority of courses and students.

COMETT, too, is well named, having flashed past our horizon bringing little in the way of funding fall-out to our students. What our students need, to be frank, is a reliable source of UK funding to support them as enterprising individuals opting for summer school courses of study abroad, or at least the return fare to encourage them to find and take summer jobs in Europe.

Assistance in finding suitable work placements and placement exchanges for students on a wide variety of courses additional to our own is given to other departments by the Languages staff. Some remission has to be given to staff from their teaching time to organise this, but that time is not recognised by the system as a drain on the departmental teaching. Now, ambitious new opportunities are to be created through the European Credit Transfer system for students of science, engineering or business to complete the middle or final parts of their course on mainland Europe. That will again create a need for more language staff involvement in the organisation and supervision of placements, and to train students well and realistically in languages before they go, presumably for all the Community languages.

What in fact will be needed is a SWITCH-type channelling of resources in favour of staffing and funding to cope with this necessary demand for languages in all sectors of education. I am certain that our competitors in Europe will be increasing their investment in the study of English by future potential exporters, as well as of other Community and more exotic languages. In Britain, our trade balance could prove very unfavourable if in the end only lip-service is paid to 1992.

November 1988

LANGUAGES IN THE UNIVERSITIES

IAN LOCKERBIE
Professor of Educational Policy and Development
University of Stirling

I hope that it will not seem over-weening or presumptious if I begin by saying that, in the spectrum of institutions and educational bodies involved in modern language teaching, the universities play a crucial role. In many ways the university sector can be seen as the lynch pin of the whole system. Not only do the universities receive, from the secondary and further education sectors, substantial numbers of students who wish to pursue foreign language studies of various kinds, they also train the vast majority of those who will eventually become the teachers of foreign languages on whom the rest of the system depends.

If, therefore, we are considering the new challenges which face foreign language teaching as an academic discipline, it is important to ask whether the training that is provided in the universities is of a kind that will equip their students to confront the demands that are likely to be made on them, either as future teachers or as graduates who will need some degree of foreign language competence among their professional skills.

Practical Skills

As far as the practical skills of language use are concerned, a survey of the situation today produces not only a reassuring picture, but a positively heartening one. There was a time when university language teaching might have been accused of lack of relevance. Twenty years ago, teaching methods were essentially based on techniques of translation - but translation restricted to a rather narrow range of language. The term often used to describe translation exercises into the foreign language - prose composition - redolent as it was of its origins in the study of ancient Latin and Greek, gives some idea of the strengths and weaknesses of the method. The strength lay in the emphasis on rigorous accuracy and sensitivity to nuances in the original text. The weakness was that it dealt with only certain styles of the language - essentially rather elevated literary styles - and left untouched many extremely relevant areas of everyday speech and writing. Notoriously, also, the spoken language was somewhat marginalised by being relegated to the province of the foreign language assistant. Not uncommonly, university teachers had no idea of how well or badly their students actually spoke the foreign language.

Since the mid-1970's, however, a veritable methodological revolution has been taking place, in which the Scottish universities have played a leading role. Although the pace and extent of change has naturally varied, courses in most institutions are now based on a much wider range of language styles, and use more diverse and stimulating methods. Not only is there greater variety in the written registers used, but the spoken language has also come in from the cold. Increasingly, in the new approaches that are being developed, comprehension and production of the spoken word are the basis on which the whole cycle of language acquisition is based. Typically students hear/see language in everyday use, before going on to tackle written exercises based on the spoken stimulus.

Modern technology has made a great contribution to the new methodologies. The use of video as a teaching instrument has brought an even greater degree of realism to language learning than the language lab, and the same is true of direct satellite broadcasting which can make contact with the foreign language environment a daily experience.

But the wonders of technology would have been of limited usefulness, had there not also been great progress in re-thinking the principles of language acquisition, and applying them in such a way as to capitalise on the new equipment. The key developments here have been in the field of applied linguistics. Serious research into the principles and practice of language learning has now become a major university discipline in its own right. No modern language department can now afford to be without specialists in this field of scholarship whose whole *raison d'être* lies in the application of fundamental research to practical improvements in methods.

These developments were not fired primarily by utilitarian objectives. The aim has been a much broader intellectual one of matching teaching more adequately to the realities of language use. But the broader conception of language competence that now underlies course provision includes an interest in vocationally relevant uses of the foreign language. No good university teacher today shrinks from the prospect of teaching language for specific purposes. On the contrary, set within the whole pattern of the new thinking about foreign language education, vocational uses of languages represent an aspect of competence that gives as much professional satisfaction to the teacher/applied linguist as any other.

As a result universities have shown increasing interest in various forms of applied language training in their degree programmes, as well as responding directly to the language requirements of industry and commerce, in initiatives such as Language Export consortia, both national and local. This is a trend that can be confidently expected to continue, particulary since the British business community, which in the past has shown itself to be woefully ignorant of the benefits of foreign language training for its personnel, is at last wakening up to the need for greater language competence. The opportunities offered by the Single European

Act of 1992 having been brought home to them, industry and commerce are now more disposed to seek out the expertise and skills of university linguists, who, for their part, are more than able and willing to respond to their needs.

Contrary to outdated assumptions, therefore, university methods in practical language teaching are now innovative and progressive in outlook. While there may be exceptions in individual institutions or individual departments, the best degree programmes provide a language training that meets the highest academic standards, while also preparing students for the practical applications of their skills that they will encounter in their future careers.

Course Structure

Where progress remains to be made is in the framework within which the improved language programmes are made available. Generally speaking, even in Scotland where, traditionally, degree structures are more flexible than in England, university courses in languages come as combined packages in which the practical study of the language is tightly wedded to the study of the culture and institutions associated with the language. The weakness of this arrangement is that it acts as a disincentive to students who simply wish to acquire a high-level command of a foreign language linked to a quite different specialisation such as business studies, computing science, chemistry, or, for that matter, English literature or philosophy. For such students the obligatory cultural components in the courses are simply not relevant to their purposes. What is required to meet their needs, but is not, on the whole, available, is a type of programme which would combine language-only courses with a chosen specialisation in a quite different field.

The reason for this inflexibility lies in the educational philosophy which has always characterised the university approach. It is a philosophy which sees language as the expression of the social and cultural environment in which it functions. It argues that to have an expert command of a foreign language (or even a fairly ordinary command) you need to know about the society which uses that language. Language expresses a world view, a set of unspoken attitudes, that are embedded in the language and are a part of how it communicates. If we do not know the cultural sub-text, we cannot grasp the full meaning.

Such a philosophy cannot be seriously challenged, so long as we are talking about the training of professional linguists to the highest levels. Language is indeed full of allusions, implications and references that cannot be picked up without a sophisticated knowledge of the cultural background of the language in question. Whether they are to be teachers, translators, interpreters or specialist linguists of any other kind, full-blown language graduates would simply be incompetently trained for their jobs if their degree programmes did not include contextual studies as well as practical language studies.

It would be stretching credibility, however, to claim that formal study of the social and cultural context is an indispensable condition for efficient language learning. Common experience tells us that many excellent linguists have acquired their competence without the benefit of cultural studies. And those universities which do provide language-only courses can testify to the high standards reached by students who take them. There seems no good reason in principle, therefore, why universities in general should not seek to make their programmes more flexible by separating out the different components in their degree schemes, and making appropriately designed language components available to students in any discipline. Nor is there any reason in principle why a sequence of such language-only units should not be part of a formal degree programme with another subject. Such programmes, which already exist in some universities, would have titles such as "Computing with Spanish language", "Business Studies with French language" or "History with German language".

Clearly, caution has to be exercised in adopting such an instrumental approach to language provision. Apart from questions of resources one reason why university language departments have traditionally fought shy of the instrumental approach is that it is dangerously close to the concept of service teaching. What is wrong with this concept is that it rests on a very mechanical notion of language, which believes that language can be supplied *ad hoc*, in random bits and pieces, as and when required. It reduces language teachers to the status of service engineers, at the beck and call of any user, without any real intellectual province of their own.

It is perhaps fear of the consequences of such crude thinking that has led some university linguists to support a special solution to the problem of supplying pragmatic language courses: that of creating separate Language Centres to undertake this task. These are excellent initiatives in their own right, and can certainly add very usefully to total language provision. But they are unsatisfactory solutions if they are allowed to become an alibi for no change in degree structures as such. It is not to the long-term advantage of language departments to remain islands of purity by shedding the pragmatic and vocational dimensions of their discipline to separate agencies. There are greater rewards to be reaped by integrating the instrumental approach into the main activities of the department, while adopting the necessary safeguards against abuse of the concept.

It is, in fact, entirely feasible, through careful course design, to steer clear of the dangers of service teaching, as the experience of some universities has shown. If stand-alone language units are introduced, these must be planned rigorously in terms of the methodologies of applied linguistics, and not simply to answer short-term user needs. If language-only units are provided as a sequence within degree programmes, access to such programmes must be controlled and monitored in such a way that they do not endanger the viability of the mainstream Honours programmes, involving contextual studies, which must remain the primary concern and activity of university departments.

What is to be gained from such controlled widening of course structures are all the advantages of breadth and diversity. Quite apart from the benefits of cross fertilisation among students, and fruitful interchange at the level of teaching methods and materials, the prospects of increased recruitment are not to be dismissed lightly. One of the unfortunate results of the prevailing, rather narrow, conception of the remit of modern languages is that it has been exlusive rather than inclusive. There are many more students in universities appropriately qualified to take modern language courses than seek to enrol - one of the reasons for their reticence being the lack of flexible course patterns. Over the last twenty years this has been one of the factors that has led to a decline in number and a relative marginalisation of modern languages within the spectrum of university disciplines.

Now there is the potential to improve on that situation. The marked developments that have taken place in the content and style of practical language courses demonstrate that we have much to offer to a more diverse audience than we have traditionally addressed. It is time to show that modern languages can be many things to many men. We no doubt cannot return to the days when a foreign language was included in the list of obligatory subjects for the ordinary MA in Scottish universities. But we can create the climate in which many students will spontaneously see it as being in their own interests to acquire a foreign language qualification within their degree studies. And we can, by a reform of structures, make it possible for them to do so.

Contextual Studies

The opening up of modern languages to a greater number of students is not the only reform we should be contemplating. Equally, we should be re-appraising the range of topics that are offered to language specialists in the traditional Honours curriculum. While there is no question about the need for a substantial diet of contextual studies for intending specialists, there are questions to be raised about the nature of these studies.

Traditionally, and still today, contextual studies have been interpreted as being essentially the study of the literature of the foreign language. Other branches of knowledge have not been ignored, of course. Some history, linguistics, and studies of contemporary society feature on the syllabus of most programmes, and tend to loom larger than such subjects did in the past. Nevertheless a glance at university calendars, and at professional journals, will show that, with the exception of the small group of so-called "technological" universities, the emphasis remains overwhelmingly on literary studies. This is, indeed, the major characteristic that distinguishes a university degree in languages from the CNAA degree schemes in polytechnics.

Without denying the value of literary study as a humane discipline from which generations of linguists have benefitted enormously, it still has to be asked whether such a concentration on this one branch of knowledge corresponds to the needs and interests of all students. Whatever may have been the case in the past, it is difficult to believe that such an emphasis is appropriate today. Recent decades have seen great changes in the nineteenth century map of knowledge, from which the rationale for the centrality of literature ultimately derives. New subjects and new approaches to understanding society have come to the fore, and indeed literary studies themselves have gone through a transformation that has made them into more of a refined specialism than the broad humanist discipline of yesteryear.

For these reasons, a review of our practice seems to be urgently called for. There is, in any case, increasing evidence of consumer resistance to the traditional diet. Various surveys have shown that more and more departments are departing from the historic framework of systematic study of literature, century by century, to concentrate their teaching on more recent and modern periods. There has been a flight from medieval, sixteenth and seventeenth century studies in search of more palatable forms of literature. In effect, a process of radical dilution of the traditional curriculum has been taking place, to the extent that it seems to have little rationale left.

What is needed, however, is not to dilute or tinker with literary studies to make them palatable, but to recognise the realities of the situation: that to concentrate on the study of literature is to offer students an excessively narrow base for the understanding of the social and cultural context of their language studies. If we believe - rightly - that an expert command of a foreign language requires an understanding of social context, then we must teach the disciplines that give that understanding as well as, or (for some students) better than, literature.

There is room for infinite diversity in the mix of disciplines which could be developed. Broadly speaking the term frequently used in CNAA degree schemes, Area Studies, indicates the conceptual framework that would be appropriate. Indeed, in so far as there are already components other than literature in university syllabuses, they tend to fall into this category. What is needed, therefore, is not a radical change of direction but a greater effort to give parity of status to those other disciplines. It is unlikely that a move in this direction would displace literature from the syllabus. It would simply provide a balanced spread of subjects, within which literature could relate meaningfully to other disciplines.

It is not an acceptable argument that students can have access to Area Studies disciplines through Combined Honours schemes with history, politics, sociology, international relations etc. A serious linguist naturally wishes to study the history and sociology of the foreign society through the medium of the foreign language itself, using foreign language materials. Nor can one appeal to a national division of labour by recommending to students with non-literary interests that they should apply for CNAA institutions. Such a free choice is not available to all students, in any case, especially in Scotland. More importantly, the argument for syllabus diversification is that a wider spectrum of disciplines is needed in all language programmes, in all institutions.

An objection sometimes made to Area Studies is that, while they promote breadth of study, they cannot provide the intellectual training in depth that comes from the specialised single or combined Honours degree schemes. But the depth/breadth antithesis seems wholly specious. It is by no means obvious that the survey courses in literary history that make up a large part of many degree schemes produce any kind of specialised knowledge worthy of the name. Nor does practising the skills of literary criticism on one or two national literatures self-evidently lead to sharper intellectual powers than studying a national culture from the point of view of the several disciplines associated with Area Studies.

On the contrary, one could argue that, in a world which is experiencing an explosion of knowledge and a rapid rate of change, a training that is multi-disciplinary is more appropriate for young people than one based on restricted specialisms. It may well be that universities generally will be faced with the need to devise more wide-ranging degree programmes than the traditional single-discipline variety, to take account of the changing nature of the intellectual challenges that the future holds. By adopting an area studies approach modern languages departments are more likely to be going in the right direction for the future than in the wrong one.

Staff Development

Many university linguists would, in fact, subscribe to the arguments for syllabus diversification but hold up the obstacle of the lack of necessary staff to teach in the new areas. It is undoubtedly true that, in the period of savage retrenchment that universities have had to contend with since 1980, modern languages have been among the areas to have suffered most. Many posts have been lost precisely at the time when the new advances in language teaching methodology have involved staff in increased workloads. Good language teaching is labour intensive, and it is becoming more so. It needs to be brought home to university managements that modern language departments have accomplished a major task in revising their teaching practices and materials in the face of great adversity, and the case for additional staff for further diversification needs to be pressed vigorously. The prospect of another round of new blood appointments may give managements an opportunity to demonstrate their understanding of the need.

At the same time realism tells us that only a proportion of the resources needed for diversification can be expected to come from new recruitment. A proportion will also have to come from redeployment of existing resources. In practice this would mean a mid-career change of orientation on the part of staff already in post, who, by personal initiatives or formal re-training, would equip themselves to add expertise in some branch of Area Studies to their existing specialisms.

Such an enterprise would add to the workload burdens, and drains on energy, from which modern language teachers already suffer. But, if properly encouraged and supported by managements, significant numbers of staff would undoubtedly rise to the challenge. Most university linguists already have a very broadly based expertise in their field of study. Through long familiarity with the environment of the languages they teach, they have precisely the multi-facetted interest in social topics, and in the issues raised by comparative cultural studies, that need to be injected into the curriculum. The problem is simply that the prevailing orthodoxy has never encouraged them to teach over as wide a range of topics as their own interests cover. It is time to put aside professional modesty and academic straitjackets. It is in the nature of modern language studies that linguists should be versatile and diverse in their skills. What is required is that the syllabuses they teach should allow them to be so.

A Watershed

University language teaching is at something of a watershed. It has been very successful in evolving with the times in the core area of its discipline. The language graduates emerging from universities are well trained linguists, with all the personal skills that come from having also had a stimulating cultural education. But the logic of the evolution that has already taken place points to the need for the kind of further developments that I have suggested.

Modern languages have the capacity to be a wider, more all-embracing discipline than they presently are. Without sacrificing present strengths, we could include within our ambit a wider spectrum of intellectual and professional skills. It is rather remarkable that, over the last twenty years, in an ever more internationally minded world, we have seen the discipline shrink and contract. There have been many contributory factors to that situation and linguists cannot take all the blame. But part of the reason undoubtedly is that we have not been broad-ranging enough to appeal to all our potential customers.

Now is the moment to cross the watershed and regain the initiative. When we see the interest that 1992 in Europe is arousing, we get the sense of how much we have to offer as a discipline, and how much we, our students and society have to gain if we go about providing our wares in the right way and in the right frame of mind.

November 1988

GAELIC: THE WAY AHEAD

ANNE LORNE GILLIES
Education Officer
Comunn na Gàidhlig

Cognitive development, intellectual flexibility, cultural awareness, mutual understanding within a multi-cultural context: the Stirling Conference constantly reaffirmed that there is far more to gain from purposeful Modern Language learning than the utilitarian rewards of commercial or vocational advancement. How ironic then that timely proposals to improve this country's linguistic profile pose practical and psychological threats to Gaelic teaching in Scottish schools. What a sad corollary if compulsory Modern Language teaching is achieved at the expense of further marginalising Gaelic in the school curriculum. But then how odd that Gaelic is not mentioned once in a Scottish conference on language teaching.

In the Government Circular on the future of language learning in Scotland (Circular 1178) Gaelic is dealt with separately from French and German: what, too ancient to be Modern? Too utopian to be European? Gaelic education sits in the solitude of its reassuring little paragraph contemplating the tenacity of its own affectionate public image as a sentimental, romantic or anachronistic exercise, worthy but irrelevant despite the establishment in recent years of new linguistic domains, wider cultural frontiers, ever increasing educational expertise and vocational opportunity.

Should we not mention Gaelic's European dimension as part of the living Celtic tradition? The international reputation of some of its living poets? Are we to believe that distinctive regional characteristics will become an embarrassment after 1992 - patently belied by unabashed minority EC cultures such as Basque and Catalan? In any case, learning Gaelic *per se* is of no less intrinsic educational value than the study of French or German, unless we argue from a crudely commercialist standpoint and ignore the intellectual and social development of the individual altogether.

The experience of Northern Ireland is instructive: though "some pupils in certain schools" have been granted the right to take Irish Gaelic in place of French or German as their compulsory language study, the pressures surrounding them will be considerable if the following ministerial statement is anything to go by: "Parents who opt for their children to learn Irish at a time when the European dimension is of growing importance should consider carefully the consequences of such a decision".

Impossible choices are nothing new to Scottish Gaels: the practice of timetabling Gaelic against French has caused successive generations of intelligent bilinguals to remain virtually illiterate in Gaelic rather than sacrifice the opportunity to apply their proven linguistic expertise to learning third and fourth languages. For able French students have traditionally progressed to take up German and/or another language at later stages, while able Gaelic students have traditionally been deprived of any such opportunities. Clearly this is unacceptable in the brave new language-orientated Scotland of the 90's - and to modern Gaelic speakers who have gained higher expectations from the changing attitudes both within and towards Gaelic education in the last few years.

For a review of some of the most recent developments reveals a significant increase in official sympathy and support for Gaelic, from the heightened awareness within the Highlands and Islands Development Board of the essential symbiotic relationship between cultural and economic regeneration, to the increasingly positive response of the Scottish Education Department and Scottish Arts Council to grassroots effort and local needs. Although Gaelic speakers remain a tiny minority in national terms (less than 100,000 living within Scotland according to the last census report, many of them demographically scattered) there has been an unprecedented sense of vibrancy and optimism as to the future of the language when compared with none too distant times, when statistics were healthier but political status and official recognition non-existent.

The reorganisation of Local Government in 1975 gave new self-confidence to the Gaelic "heartland" through the creation of *Comhairle nan Eilean*, the two-tier Western Isles Islands Council (WIIC). This found expression in the use of the native language for all official business within the Council, and in repercussions throughout education, local economy and the social services. Notable was the official designation of the Western Isles and, later, parts of Highland Region, as a bilingual area as regards primary school education: primary teachers were required to be Gaelic speakers, all primary age children to be educated through the medium of Gaelic for a substantial portion of each day.

A Gaelic Higher Education College (*Sabhal Mòr Ostaig*), teaching and examining Business Studies through the medium of Gaelic, was established in Skye, independently run but with substantial official grant aid. The College is gradually extending its remit, but persists in the practical business orientation of its full-term validated courses, which now include Information Technology and Office Technology, with Media Studies among courses planned for the future. These initiatives have in their turn spawned many offshoots: the Gaelic College, for example, is developing a Gaelic computer data-base, while WIIC has funded valuable educational research and development, including teaching resources, computer software, Gaelic Communications modules and distance learning.

In 1982 a charitable organisation for the establishment of Gaelic-medium play groups - *Comhairle nan Sgoiltean Araich* (CNSA) - was set up and has won official grant-aid at both national and local levels. Demand has risen consistently for this type of pre-school provision, and CNSA now functions as a professionally run coordinating body for an ever increasing number of playgroups throughout Scotland, the beginnings of a similar movement in Canada, and a mobile project (or play bus) which is made available to any area on request.

Around 1,000 children attend the Gaelic playgroups, including large numbers from non-Gaelic-speaking homes - especially in the cities and areas outwith the *Gaidhealtachd*. SED funding underwrites central administration, resource development, publishing, training etc, while Regional Authorities give direct assistance to many CNSA branches and local based projects. More recently Regional Education Authorities have begun appointing their own pre-school officers to complement and develop the work of CNSA, and one Region has embarked upon official Gaelic nursery school provision. However, the everyday running, staffing and funding of the playgroups depends on voluntary parental and community effort. Active parental involvement has become an important catalyst, bringing women back into the workforce, increasing awareness of educational theory and practice, and, latterly, encouraging demand for a continuation of Gaelic-medium education into the mainstream primary school sector. There are twelve Gaelic-medium Units housed within primary schools in different parts of Scotland, rising to around twenty in the 1989-90 session.

Their steady increase has been encouraged through a Government scheme of Specific Grants for Gaelic which effectively sets Gaelic education outwith the local political arena of competing demands and priorities, and provides Regional Authorities with the means to apply a degree of positive discrimination to Gaelic in response to present parental demand. Future levels for the Specific Grant are partly based on each local authority's forecast of its own likely needs, and partly on cooperative Inter-Authority initiatives (in-service teacher training, large scale resource development etc) a process which has encouraged collaboration between Regions to a degree which must be almost unique within the present educational system. This creates a mechanism for long term-planning, a forum within which to discuss the implications for Gaelic of wider educational issues - a valuable asset for a language with no official legal status within its own country of origin.

Another such mechanism has been added through the establishment of *Comunn na Gàidhlig* (CNAG) - a national agency funded through the Scottish Office and remitted to coordinate and service Gaelic initiatives, both mainstream and voluntary. CNAG has been instrumental in forming a network of Gaelic-medium youth clubs, where the work of the schools is developed into the areas of leisure and recreation. Government support has extended into other vital areas such as Gaelic book publishing and radio broadcasting, and a properly funded, legally protected Scottish Gaelic television service is presently under discussion as part of Government plans for the future of British broadcasting.

However, Gaelic education remains highly vulnerable - not so much to legislation aimed specifically at the language as to the oblique effects of general national educational measures - much harder to shift in the direction of a minority, however great the general goodwill. Several such landmines are planted in the current wide-ranging legislative proposals - doubtless without any malice aforethought as to their possible effects in this particular field with its new sown seeds. Compulsory Modern Language study, and the built-in self-fulfilling implication that Gaelic has less relevance in the wider European context, is the most obviously pertinent to this discussion. But it is equally important to address some of the other proposals and their possible implications for Gaelic education.

School Boards for example. The Gaelic-medium Units are housed within larger primary schools and, especially in the cities, draw children from very wide catchments. Parents thus have much less chance of getting to know one another, let alone parents in the rest of the school, to assure themselves of representation on the Boards. For the purposes of election Gaelic parents are to be treated as ordinary members of a whole-school society. Yet the education being offered to their children is highly specialised, has special aims and needs which should be represented.

This presents an even more perturbing aspect with the probability of schools becoming permitted to opt out of Authority control in the future, especially when we consider the vital role currently being played by individual Regional Authorities in supporting local Gaelic initiatives, and in cooperative Inter-Authority measures. In the absence of any detailed national policy on Gaelic education, such cooperation is vital in areas like resource development and teacher training and supply (both matters of grave concern even for the immediate future) and any fragmentation of our small-scale but highly effective *status quo* could be extremely damaging.

Assessment of primary school children also has implications for Gaelic-medium education. Small children who have acquired their initial literacy skills in Gaelic immersion classes are unlikely to be ready for assessment through the medium of English by Primary 4, though by Primary 7 the disparity will have been evened out. Will exception be made for such children? Gaelic-medium testing devices produced? Or will teachers begin erring on the side of safety (i.e. English) to the detriment of the children's progress in Gaelic? Testing of such young children is in any case bound to emphasise the widely varying speeds at which all infants develop, in any classroom. But in the case of Gaelic-medium education differing extramural language exposure is liable to amplify these variations in the test results of certain children and within certain schools.

One might say that the range and remit of present proposals is spreading uncertainty and qualms among all parents, whatever their circumstances. But after many generations of learning to view their own language as a disadvantage in educational, vocational and economic terms, it is almost impossible to exaggerate the sensitivity of Gaelic speakers to adverse influences: thus parental confidence and pupil uptake could be quite disproportionately affected by any or all of the foregoing. Fear of poor test results, for example, may haunt any future parent of a small child: in terms of Gaelic-medium education such fears, however unfounded, might empty the classrooms.

And the same vulnerability can all too easily extend beyond the uncertainties of individual parents to affect whole areas of policy. The Western Isles Bilingual Project, for example, was subjected to an untimely moratorium for independent external assessment at the very stage when the first generation of bilingually educated children was about to transfer to island secondary schools, thus thwarting the anticipated natural progression of the Project into the secondary sector. This unfortunate situation has prevailed ever since, despite the positive findings subsequently published by the external assessment team. A modicum of Gaelic-medium teaching has existed in junior secondary schools where Gaelic is the first language of the majority of staff and pupils, and there is a healthy uptake of Gaelic as a subject in Island secondary schools. However, this falls far short of an official secondary Gaelic-medium teaching programme - in the Gaelic heartland, with the highest concentration of bilingual pupils to benefit from it and Gaelic speaking teachers to staff it.

Conversely, Strathclyde Regional Council has already taken the first steps towards employing Gaelic as a teaching medium in some secondary school curricular areas - only three years after it embarked on Gaelic-medium primary education. Small numbers are involved - the children transferring to one Glasgow secondary school from the related Bilingual Primary Unit - but the repercussions have already been far-reaching: the Scottish Examination Board has agreed to the principle of examining, in Gaelic, subjects which have been studied through the medium of the language - a major step forward in officially acknowledging the viability of the language.

Significantly, the same Glasgow secondary school has proved that, where the political will exists, the timetable can be juggled to include the teaching of Gaelic as a subject without loss of other available language options. All the bilingual pupils (at present in Secondary 1) are studying English, Gaelic, French and German - a situation which would nowadays be unremarkable in Wales, or in any of the European countries with official minority language policies, but which is another major achievement in Gaelic terms.

It would seem important, therefore, that educationalists and politicians alike project a view of the "way forward" for language teaching in Scotland which at every stage and in every detail includes the Gaelic dimension; which clearly recognises and caters for the four distinct levels on which Gaelic functions within the education system:

a. Gaelic as a **means of communication** - a teaching medium for bilinguals within the Gaelic Units, and in informal exchanges between staff and pupils in some secondary schools (i.e. equivalent to English as used in parallel situations)

b. Gaelic as a discrete **language/literature/communications subject-area** - presently conceived as the "native speaker Gaelic course" (i.e. equivalent to English as a subject taught to all Scottish secondary school pupils)

c. Gaelic as a **Second Language** - as taught to monolingual primary children through Immersion Programmes in the Gaelic Units (i.e. equivalent to ESL induction programmes for immigrant children in Language Centres) and

d. Gaelic as a **Modern Language** - as taught to non-Gaelic- speaking pupils in secondary schools and F.E. classes, and presently conceived as the "learners' Gaelic course" (i.e. equivalent to French or German or any other Modern/Foreign Language). Also as taught by peripatetic specialists in a few primary schools (i.e. equivalent to French or German in the current proposals).

Recognition of these distinct functions is essential if Gaelic is to acquire proper status and Gaelic teachers to be presented with pre-service training programmes appropriate to their intended careers. At present, ordinary primary teachers who happen to be bilingual are employed in Gaelic Units and handle immersion programmes, late arrivals, learning difficulties and resource development without any specialist language training whatsoever; secondary Gaelic specialists have to cover all the areas normally handled by at least two, possibly three equivalent departments (English, Modern Languages and, arguably, History - as Highland history has traditionally been so neglected in the national syllabus, even in Highland schools).

In recent years, Gaelic has proved itself as flexible and adaptable to new concepts and vocabulary as any other twentieth century language. Its speakers have proved themselves capable of enormous sustained effort in terms of self-help, receptive to assistance and new ideas. It is a useful language which means as much to Gaelic speakers as English does to the English (or Scots!) But numerically and psychologically Gaelic is disadvantaged. All Gaelic speakers are nowadays bilingual; but the Dutch can conduct their business transactions in English or sing along with the American pop stars without wondering whether they ought to stop teaching their own language to their own children in order to get them through their tests or make them better citizens of the EC.

With uncertainty hanging over future developments in almost every aspect of education today, Gaelic educationalists must be able to count on the support and understanding of their colleagues in other Language Departments - to ensure that the recent, hard-won recognition of the importance of language (to the individual and to society) extends its protective cloak to embrace Gaelic language and culture too. For even if the re-introduction of French or German into the primary school classroom founders, or compulsory language learning produces no significant rise in the communicative skills of the general populace of Scotland, French or German will continue to flourish in France and Germany, new French and German books and records will continue to appear for the delectation of Scottish Modern Languages teachers, French and German cuisine will still be available for the gourmet tourist, and the satellite dish will prove that French and German popular culture is alive and well in its place of origin. But Scotland is Gaelic's country of origin and the whole future of Gaelic culture in all its aspects hangs upon the success of current educational measures in Scottish schools to produce another generation of Gaelic speakers from under the mighty nose of the Anglo-American monster.

And such support and understanding would be mutually enhancing - for Gaelic education could be a valuable source of information for Modern Language teachers implementing the new policies, especially in the field of primary school language teaching. Peripatetic Gaelic speakers, typically secondary trained, have been operating in primary schools in the north and west (especially Highland Region) since the 1960's, teaching the language as a discrete subject to monolingual children and, more recently, integrating it into the work of the school. Although their work has been valuable in increasing awareness, both linguistic and cultural, among large numbers of children, it has not had a significant effect on the skills or motivation of pupils entering the secondary school and movement tends now towards the replacement of "a little language teaching for all" with concentration of effort in: a. the special Gaelic-medium Primary Units (as already described) and b. a much smaller number of recently designated bilingual primary schools in Highland Region, where the effort of peripatetic language specialists will be more concentrated - in closer cooperation with class teachers and for longer periods of time, operating in cross-curricular fashion and encouraging the class teacher to continue the process at other times.

Welsh experience is also highly relevant here, especially in Gwynedd, where the peripatetic specialists (*Athrawon Bro*) now work in teams, inhabiting whole schools for a term or more, teaching alongside existing staff in every classroom, and providing what is in effect a substantial period of in-service training in communicative methods and the integration of language into the primary school curriculum. In this way, teachers are encouraged to use what linguistic skills they possess (usually far greater than they fear) instead of leaving it all to the visiting "Welsh ladies" as before. And the children grow up recognising language as a method of meaningful communication for everybody rather than an academic exercise at which some are doomed to fail.

Experience in Gaelic-medium education is also of immediate relevance to the teaching of French or German in Scottish schools. A surprisingly high proportion of the children involved in this type of education begin school as monolinguals and have little access to extramural linguistic back-up, especially in the cities. Therefore, a considerable period of initial language immersion is necessary, combining stimulating activities with sustained and relevant language input; and even then passive skills considerably precede productive, just as in any French or German classroom.

A most palpable difference from any other Modern Language situation, however, lies in the relative scarcity of Gaelic resources (unimaginable to teachers in other areas) and the unavailability of relevant pre-service training for Gaelic-medium teachers. The success and variety of their stratagems indicate not only their personal commitment and skill as teachers and instinctive communicators, but also the intrinsic advantages of this type of language programme. For infant classrooms provide a microcosm within which almost every human activity (acceptable and anti-social, intellectual and practical, real-life and imaginary) takes place naturally in the course of the school day - a polymorphous situational language environment such as specialist language teachers working with older children can only dream of or attempt to emulate in self-conscious role-play.

Again, the linguistic outcomes implicit in Gaelic-medium education are almost identical to those explicitly stated in any communicative language course. Indeed a number of parents who opt for Gaelic-medium education are motivated primarily by the desire for their children to become bilingual and enjoy all-round experience of an alternative culture - no matter what the Second Language or culture. This also indicates the growing awareness that early bilingualism facilitates the acquisition of third and fourth languages. Perhaps the future provision in selected schools of similar Modern (and so-called Community) Language

Immersion Units might provide an even more potent solution to our chronic monoculturalism than discrete language lessons for all ten-year-olds.

Indeed, perhaps we should consider establishing designated "language schools", where immersion programmes in several different languages could flourish side by side. Worries about representation on School Boards, or opting out of Authority control, or integration in whole-school activities fade before a sudden vision of multilingual school assemblies, with Gaelic taking its proper place alongside the other Modern European Languages.

May 1989

JAPANESE TEACHING IN SCOTTISH SCHOOLS

I GOW
Professor and Director of the Scottish Centre for Japanese Studies
University of Stirling

Over the last three decades Japan has emerged as a major trading nation. She now shows signs of becoming a major power technologically and scientifically. In addition she has now emerged as the world's largest creditor nation and the new financial superpower. Tokyo is now a key element in global economic and increasingly political policy. Her export successes in overseas markets have now been followed by an increased financial and manufacturing presence in all major industrial economies. Yet for all of that she remains the most mysterious and indeed the most misunderstood nation. This is in part due to her culture but also to the formidable language barrier. Whether one wishes to compete, collaborate or learn from Japan we desperately need a massive qualitative increase in the data available on this dynamic country. This knowledge base must be made available at all levels within our educational system and it seems both obvious and highly sensible that our children are provided with the tools to understand better the phenomenon called Japan. In this context one needs to see developments in the curriculum for most school subjects which incorporate elements, units or modules on Japan, especially contemporary Japan.

Given Japan's present position and a possible strengthening of that position, one might also add that there is a perceived need for not only the development and expansion of Japanese studies but also Japanese language in the schools curriculum. The recent Parker Report on Oriental Languages (1987) highlighted the shortage of expertise on Japan required for commercial and diplomatic relations and, as a result, the University Grants Committee made available more funding for Japanese Studies and especially Japanese language at university level. The Department of Trade and Industry also recently announced (April 1989) that 1.6 million pounds are to be made available to higher education institutions for developing language training for business purposes. However, despite the professed enthusiasm for foreign languages amongst policy makers, little progress has been made in the provision of central funding for the teaching of Japanese in schools. The DES, in its recent categorisation, has made Japanese a category 2 language but extensive lobbying had brought little more than vague statements and the pioneering work in Japanese language in schools has been left to a few individuals with limited funding.

The Centre for Japanese Studies at Stirling University, founded in 1981, can be said to have pioneered teaching and research on Japanese for schools. In particular Centre staff, in conjunction with Richard Johnstone of Stirling's Department Education, developed and successfully obtained approval for a 40 hour SCOTVEC module in Japanese and this was taught at Stirling High School and Balwearie High School. Funding, by a consortium of Scottish firms, enabled the Centre's Japanese lecturer (Setsuko Wakabayashi) to allocate part of her time to testing the SCOTVEC module and carry out research on language acquisition amongst schoolchildren. The project achieved its aims and the module continues to be offered, but with reduced assistance from the Centre for Japanese Studies.

In 1987 the Centre for Japanese Studies received major funding from the UGC and today, with a totally new staff and major corporate funding and research grants, has expanded and has been officially recognised as the Scottish Centre for Japanese Studies by the Secretary of State for Scotland. As the national centre it is intended to act as a major resource for expanding the study of Japan throughout the educational sector. In developing our planning however, our major resources were directed away from schools to university level undergraduate and postgraduate teaching and the first ever honours degree programmes at a Scottish University are now being taught at Stirling. One might well then ask what happened to Stirling's commitment to teaching on Japanese in schools. One immediate answer is that the pilot project was over, no government funding was made available and the centre's priorities were allocated to other areas. That would be misleading although not without an element of truth. We are enthusiastic about teaching Japanese language and civilisation in schools but only under conditions which ensure that the language elements are well resourced and, more importantly, well taught. On the Japanese studies side we recently hosted a one day teach-in for geography teachers in the Central Region, partially funded by the Embassy of Japan, partially by the University, and 68 teachers attended. We know therefore that there is considerable enthusiasm for teaching Japanese studies in schools and the Embassy will help with schools projects and even offers trips to Japan for primary and secondary teachers carrying out Japan-related projects in their classes.

Japanese language teaching in schools has an almost immediate appeal. There is considerable activity in England, in the state and private sectors, and Wales is now looking to develop Japanese in schools. Given the increased presence of Japanese companies in Scotland together with Japan's penetration of all facets of UK economic life, it certainly is a useful foreign language and would undoubtedly increase job prospects if proficiency were attained. The first major problem however is how to find the space to effectively develop competence in one of the world's acknowledged difficult languages within an already crowded syllabus. Above all, Japanese is a language which requires greater time than other modern languages. A place could be found, no doubt, but again, at the expense of which subject, or indeed which other foreign language? The development of the 40 hour SCOTVEC module shows that some Japanese, within a relatively standardised curriculum, can be taught and indeed can be added to a syllabus within Scottish schools without the major resource implications of Standard Grade/Higher subject development. However given the time available, as well as the concentration on written as well as spoken Japanese, achievement levels are understandably very basic. In England generic modular framework-based Japanese units have been prepared for Suffolk Graded Examinations in Modern Languages and the GCSE Syllabus and there is also now a Cambridge Certificate in Japanese. There has however been no major debate, and certainly no major research from the Japanese centres regarding the ideal syllabus or indeed whether Japanese can simply be designed under generic Modern language guidelines. The older "O" and "A" level Japanese (London) is in need of considerable revision and is overwhelmingly taken by Japanese nationals resident in the UK (surely not the original intention one feels). Much work needs to be done in this area.

Next there is the problem of resources. Any new resources for foreign languages would, and indeed should, first be allocated to remedy the attrition in other modern languages over the last decade or so, so that we can again boast a schools curriculum which is adequately resourced for two or even one foreign language. Only when it could be clearly shown that languages where we do have considerable expertise and need (eg EEC languages) are not having potential new funding diverted to Japanese should we then think of allocating funding to Japanese. Japanese should not replace other crucially important modern languages, it should be added to the list. Funding however is only one resource problem. The other is teaching expertise.

The new Parker posts in Japanese studies and the creation of new regional UGC-funded Centres in Scotland, Wales and the North of England, whilst welcome, highlighted the dearth of high quality candidates for teaching Japanese language and Japanese Studies. This reflected the massive reduction in postgraduate studies on Japan over the last decade as resources were withdrawn in the face of government cuts. There is therefore, within the UK, a shortage of suitably qualified candidates for existing vacancies in Japanese Studies.

Assuming adequate resourcing, and availability of time in the curriculum, where would schools obtain the staffing to teach Japanese in schools? The UK at present produces only around 55 graduates in Japanese a year. They are snapped up by business or are attracted to take up various kinds of employment in Japan. Rarely do they become school teachers. The number of graduates is due to double within the next five years and this may provide some recruits to teaching although at present there are signs that other more lucrative employment will expand to meet this new supply.

A second potential source of teachers is provided by returnee English teachers from Japan. The most important source of these is the Japan English Teachers Scheme (JETS) originated by a Mr Nicholas Wolfers in conjunction with the Japanese Embassy in London. This provides employment opportunities for UK graduates to teach English in Japan in schools, universities or companies etc. The numbers are increasing annually and now over 150 a year are despatched for periods of one to two years. Many of these return and enter the teaching profession and are often, naturally, enthusiasts for Japanese studies and sometimes Japanese language developments in the curriculum of their school. The problem, especially where Japanese language is concerned, is that despite perhaps a familiarity with techniques related to teaching English as a Foreign Language, they seldom have achieved a high enough level of Japanese to adequately teach the subject at school. Given that they were English teachers in Japan, rarely with any formal study of the language, and given the Japanese hunger for practising English, it would take a remarkable young teacher with a will of iron, to create the opportunities to achieve any real competence. Graduates returning from teaching English in Japan do add to our pool of knowledge on things Japanese in schools and elsewhere but in the main simply confirm the fears of many Japan specialists that enthusiasm is being confused with competence.

A third category of potential teachers is composed of native speakers of Japanese. There is now an increasing number of Japanese nationals (wives of businessmen, students etc) available in this country. Many of the wives are indeed graduates and many may have teaching certificates. Indeed SCOTVEC regulations require native speakers to have appropriate teaching qualifications. However teaching qualifications in general and those required for teaching Japanese (as a second language) are quite a different matter. One scheme advocated by some influential people in Anglo-Japanese relations is to utilise Japanese teachers in the UK studying English to be assigned to schools to teach Japanese. This again looks very promising but again assumes that teachers of English can double as teachers of Japanese. Dr Miriam Jellinek of Sheffield's Centre for Japanese Studies, has advocated that native teachers of Japanese ought to have training and qualifications in teaching Japanese as a second language. This is clearly not the case at present in Japanese teaching in schools, in extra mural teaching and indeed even within many Japan centres. Native speakers of the language, properly trained in second language acquisition skills, would be a tremendous asset and, even without that training, if guided and assisted by native speakers of English with competence in Japanese could be a marvellous resource. Funding for short courses and support materials for native speakers in teaching Japanese in schools would certainly help, along with a commonly agreed syllabus and good teaching materials. However so far this has not been offered or suggested and indeed we have not been approached directly by any local, regional or national authority for advice or suggestions in this area (other than for the SCOTVEC pilot project).

Given the shortage of funding and qualified teachers, I feel that rushing forward with schemes for developing Japanese at the schools level may be somewhat premature, especially in view of the need to respond to new (if under-resourced) initiatives on modern European languages. Badly taught Japanese modules may create problems for universities when these students go on to higher education. Whilst the Centre for Japanese Studies at Stirling University is keen to support language teaching in schools it is certainly not our primary responsibility which is to the university sector. That responsibility would be undermined if scarce resources were allocated to teaching language in schools. A major initiative in schools especially in the language area would, under the present system, undoubtedly stretch our existing resources beyond acceptable limits.

Much of the above may well sound rather pessimistic especially to those people in the schools system who advocate teaching of Japanese. I would respond by stating that the Centre for Japanese Studies has already shown its commitment to schools, through the SCOTVEC development (we are the designated examination centre) and through our teachers workshops. Given that our priority lies with university education, we would suggest the following development plan for teaching Japanese and Japanese studies in schools.

First, since resources available for schools teaching are absent, we would suggest that teaching of Japanese language beyond short taster courses should be done within the university sector at present. As a University Centre, we could then allocate resources to the teaching of Japanese Studies within teacher training programmes whilst simultaneously developing modules to be incorporated within existing school examination syllabi. We certainly believe that trainee teachers can be effectively taught courses on modern and contemporary Japan over a relatively short period. This is certainly not the case with Japanese language. We can also provide, in conjunction with the Japanese Embassy, a resource base for curriculum development. As the number of graduates in Japanese curriculum studies from Stirling and elsewhere increases, so the pool of competent teachers can be expanded. We would then, if the programmes in schools were developed and successful, provide in-service summer school training for existing teachers. All of this, we would hope, would greatly expand our children's knowledge of Japan and hopefully persuade many of them to go on and study Japan at a higher level and to study the Japanese language at Stirling or elsewhere. We do see the possibilities of summer schools for children, Saturday schools in central locations for groups of schools and taster courses on Japanese studies and language as well as occasional lectures at schools throughout Scotland. We are now creating a major Japanese library resource at Stirling as well as superb audio-visual materials and we do see this as a major resource available to schools. We are engaged in major multi-country research initiatives on second language acquisition of Japanese as well as curriculum design and will be expanding this to include schools level development. Our new language specialists, grounded in a different approach to Japanese than past staff, eagerly look forward to the opportunity of working with the Education Department at Stirling University, with colleges of education and with enlightened education authorities.

April 1989

FOREIGN LANGUAGES IN BUSINESS

SIR GERALD ELLIOT
Chairman
Christian Salvesen plc

I belong to a company which over the years operated as much outside the UK as inside. When we were in Antarctic whaling, Norwegian was our trading language, and for operating reasons a language we had to know. Later we went to Peru and ran a fishmeal business. There, of course, we worked in Spanish. Pretty few fishmeal people knew any English, and those who knew English didn't know fishmeal. Nothing concentrates the mind more than arriving at a fish plant, seeing everything run appallingly and having only a drunken, ignorant and obstinate Scots mechanic available to transfer operating requirements to Peruvian managers.

Since the mid 1970's, the company has been increasingly involved on the continent of Europe, first France, then Belgium, then Holland, finally Germany - now quite heavily there. Our main activities are cold storage and transport. Each company runs independently, but there are many links with the home office on the technical and marketing sides. We do have other businesses, oilfield technology and generator hire, which run in those countries and in Norway and Finland, but these are smaller units and report directly to central management in the UK.

On the basis of this experience, you have asked me what language skills are required for Scottish business and how the educational system might help to provide them.

The ideal must be for every staff member who is going to deal with these foreign operations, from chairman downwards, to have a working knowledge of the languages, or at the least the major ones, French and German. At operating level you have to have the language to pass over your own knowhow - that is often the main reason for making a foreign investment. Further up it is much more difficult to integrate managers and get them working in harmony if there are language barriers; and at policy level you must know what makes another country tick, what's happening in business, what the trends are, who are the crooks. It is very difficult to do this unless you can read the newspapers and converse freely with people. Of course, many continental managers are fluent in English, and will negotiate in English. But because there is always work to be done in French and German, they will have the practical and psychological edge on you, if you cannot produce the same language knowledge. Our rule has been to have a local national in charge of our business in these countries, or a bilingual Britisher, so that within the local company no language barriers exist. But there is still the possible obstacle between

HQ and local companies because of language ignorance. We found that in Belgium and Holland we were successful from the start. In France, we had troubles for many years. I attribute that very largely to the language ignorance of our Britishers concerned with France, which stopped us getting on top of our very chauvinist French manager. In contrast there was a high degree of language competence in Holland and Flemish Belgium, where all the managers and many of the other staff spoke good English.

We know that people in smaller countries are better at languages than in larger. There is a very high knowledge of English in Sweden, Norway, Holland, Flemish Belgium. They all realise they are going to have to make a living dealing with foreigners and that the foreigners won't bother to learn their language. Of course, English is the primary world language, so they learn it first. This is even more necessary in Finland, where a considerable effort has to be made to learn a language completely outside the Western European mainstream. We have a similar small country in Scotland, where we have to work particularly hard to make a living, and have to make it dealing with foreigners. But we naturally find the easiest foreigners in England, so there is no special urge to acquire other languages. There is a sentimental view that Scots are more disposed to acquire languages that the English. I have yet to see much evidence on that score. But we do know that we aren't self-sufficient and have always traded our skills all over the world as well as with England, and it may be that this will make us more conscious of overseas markets, and perhaps make us work harder to be good linguists.

I said the ideal was to have everyone involved overseas bilingual or trilingual. I am afraid we, in our company, fall very short of that. When we started into the continent of Europe, the people we would have wanted to put in there were sound middle managers to senior managers in their late 30's and early 40's. None of them knew a word of French or German, or, if they had learnt any at school, had forgotten it all. We had recruited and developed them to run our business in the UK, and they weren't prepared for anything else. Some have learned a language since, but few of them at all convincingly. We encouraged them strongly and sent them on courses. I ran a French table at lunch in our canteen for some months. Overall we are now much stronger than we were, because in recent recruiting we have looked for some language fluency as a necessary qualification, but most of these people are still quite junior. People don't usually set about learning languages for fun, but I think that as they see more of our management opportunites coming up in Europe they will get down to it, assisted by pressure from their seniors.

That is the picture of our company, probably fairly typical, though we may be suffering more strains through fairly fast expansion. Our needs were, in the previous generation, Norwegian and then Spanish. Now they are French and German. Of course, Russian will be needed as Eastern Europe opens up, and there must be some Japanese speakers to meet those formidable people on their own terms. I should think that for most companies, with 1992 coming up, French and German will take equal first priority, with Spanish a close third.

What useful thoughts flow from all this for education? For business purposes we need people who are fluent in speaking, understanding and reading a language, in addition to the more general skills of management, which they may bring or we may provide them with. We in business have, of course, high responsibility to teach our people the skills they need for the job, but we should also look to the educational system of the country to help on languages, which anyway give social and cultural benefit as well as industrial.

I am ignorant of the structure and content of existing university and technical college courses, so I can only make tentative suggestions as to how this business demand might be met. Universities already do modern language courses, but we are not looking for that degree of specialisation. Indeed, our prescription is really for technical instruction to be added to an academic degree. It is really just a basic skill, to be acquired as part of the necessary business equipment - a tool of communication like computing. Could this not be done with economics, or law, or engineering, or business studies? Or perhaps an intensive three month course post degree with the help of language labs and other modern supports? There could also be more mixed degrees. I am sure that the tertiary system can devise courses on these lines, perhaps have already, particularly when the demand comes, not in general terms from business companies, but individually from students, who increasingly will come to realise that this is a skill they must have.

I don't think it is worth paying people extra to learn languages as part of company policy. You don't need everyone in the organisation to be linguists, and those concerned will get recognition by promotion anyway. This should be enough to interest staff in acquiring a language.

Our relative incompetence in foreign languages goes back beyond tertiary education into secondary and even primary education. How is it that while most educated Continentals are fluent in at least English, most similar English and Scots are fluent in nothing, even if they have taken an "O" level at school, and speak with great embarrassment and appalling accent? It is a wholly different culture, and we can only change this by starting young. We should be getting kids to chatter naturally in French almost before they read and write. If we can train Suzuki violin players, who not Suzuki German speakers? If they start early, they will speak a live language, not a painfully constructed exercise, and will instinctively correct their accents by mimicry. I know that teachers must put first the basic literacy and arithmetic skills that are necessary for economic survival in the present world. But there must be a fairly large proportion of children who could absorb a language at an early age in addition to everything else and keep it fresh for adult life. I shall be most interested to hear the latest view on the teaching of languages. I am sure techniques are being continually improved.

Why is it we all speak with such bad accents? At least 80% of people have a musical ear - can learn and sing songs tunefully - but most are quite unable to transfer skill to languages. I think it must be because they begin with the written word and transfer it into English sounds, then can't be brought back on the right track.

Not all industrial companies are going to need linguists. Some will continue to cultivate only the UK market; others will judge that they can run their limited overseas business without high language skills; but many, and particularly as the European market integrates, will have to have far more expertise than they have at present. I hope that this conference will provide some help.

November 1988

NOTES ON BALLANTYNE'S FOREIGN LANGUAGE POLICY

ANN L. RYLEY
Sales and Merchandising Manager
Ballantyne Sportswear, Innerleithen

First of all, a short profile of Ballantyne. We are a company within the Dawson Group, manufacturing high quality predominantly Cashmere but also fine wool knitwear for men and women. We have two factories, one in Innerleithen, Peebleshire, one in Bonnyrigg, near Edinburgh; and we employ a total of 650 people. In addition, we have a range of clothing including jackets, suits and trousers made under licence in Italy which enables us to present to customers a "total look". Our turnover this year was £20 million. 70% of our turnover is direct exports; and even business in London, due to the high price of our product, is to tourists rather than British customers. Our main export markets in descending order of importance are as follows:- Italy, Japan/Far East, France, Germany, Switzerland. Spain is a small market at present but we anticipate growth.

We mainly work through Agents who are nationals based in their respective market, and earn commission on sales. Our sales are to individual up-market shops rather than store groups, which means we have a large number of customers in each market.

Our staff with language ability are as follows:-

Marketing Director - Working and good knowledge of French and German.
Sales and Merchandising Manager - Degree in French and German from Bradford University. Since joining Ballantyne has learnt Italian. Also, until recently, another Sales Manager with German, Spanish and Russian learnt in the RAF. He has since left but we will be looking to recruit a language graduate to train. (See advertisment below)
Secretary to Marketing Director - Ordinary degree from Glasgow University (major subjects : French and Italian). Higher German.

Ways in which languages are used

Marketing Director
- Talking to Agents and customers in person and on the telephone. Reading correspondence and trade journals.

Secretary to Marketing Director
- Typing letters in foreign language. Translating letters/reports/documents

from and into foreign language. Occasionally speaking to Agents/customers on the telephone.

Sales and Merchandising Manager
- Talking to cusomers in person and on the telephone.
- Talking to Agents in person and on the telephone.
- Writing to customers/Agents.
- Recently, as Ballantyne have formed a Company in France and opened their own shop there:- talking and corresponding with lawyers, bank, accountant, French authorities, and translating legal texts and balance sheets.
- Checking promotional material and video text in foreign language in conjunction with native speakers/Agents.
- Translating correspondence which has to be actioned e.g. by Sales Service Department.
- Liaising with our clothing manufacturer in Italy.
Languages are in daily use by all three members of staff.

What benefits do we derive from our foreign language policy?

1. Both the Marketing Director and Sales and Merchandising Manager travel frequently to visit our Agents. Most speak fluent English, but obviously tend to express themselves more easily in their native tongue, so communication with Agents is facilitated.
2. We visit our customers regularly. Speaking to customers in their own language has numerous advantages.
   a. We must remember we are selling a product the customer must feel at ease to want to buy. He does so most when speaking his native tongue. In speaking the language you make an effort for him, and this is appreciated.
   b. Although most of our Agents could act as interpreters, they are not qualified to do so and they may only interpret their views of the customer's needs. Speaking the customer's language is the only way not to be totally dependent on your Agent.
   c. In fashion, it is most important to be close to the customer in order to be able to interpret fashion trends in that market and react quickly. Speaking the language is the only way to be able to carry out such market research and a basic knowledge of the culture/habits/mentality of each market is vital. This can only be gained by speaking the language. This also immediately shows the customer you understand his needs.
   Quote from my German Agent: "You can't possibly speak German so well as you do without having an interest and understanding of the country".

d. Follow-up. The customer needs to know he can 'phone/write and be replied to in his own language for problems of delivery/development/quality problems.

e. It gives you the edge over your competitors, most of whom cannot speak the language. Customers are often surprised to find business men or women from the UK with language ability.

f. Social/entertaining - enables you to spend time socially with your customers, which always brings you closer.

3. When we recently formed our company in France, this exercise did not involve our Agent. In the South of France, we did not find lawyers, accountants or bank managers with any knowledge of English; therefore our languages were vital.

4. Occasionally languages are used to communicate with suppliers. In this case, I always feel the supplier should speak our language as we are then the customer, but this is not always the case.

5. Very few people at our clothing manufacturer in Italy speak English. Closer relations have grown through me learning Italian which has lead to a more efficient service from them.

6. Information - reading trade journals etc.

7. Organising our participation at exhibitions abroad.

Experience abroad

I have personally had experience of working abroad, in the electronics sector, and have seen the reactions of foreign firms to British companies with no language capabilities. One major contract was being negotiated whilst I was working in France for CGEE Alsthom in Belfort, France. A French company was trying for the contract, as was a German one with French speakers, and a British company. It was made quite clear to me that if the products offered were the same and of similar price, only French speakers stood a chance of the contract. Each time anyone from the British company visited, CGEE Alsthom had to pay me to interpret and translate documents. They were obviously also concerned about after sales service and communication. The British company lost the contract. This was not an isolated case. The onus is on the company selling to speak the language of its customer.

Example of advertisement for Sales/Merchandising Manager

Further particulars: We currently wish to augment our Sales/Marketing Team by engaging one high calibre person initially based in the Scottish Borders.

Reporting to the Marketing Director, candidates for this appointment, male or female and probably aged 25-35, will be required to establish and maintain close contact with the Company's Agents and Customers internationally. In addition they will be required to identify, source and control other items complementary to the primary product.

Fluency in at least two European languages, combined with a knowledge of culture and customs of the relevant countries, is mandatory for all applicants. Whilst not essential, experience in the Quality Fashion Clothing sector, either in a wholesale or retail capacity, will be an advantage.

Of primary importance is the ability to meet and deal with discerning quality conscious customers and suppliers. Considerable foreign travel will be required.

October 1988

THE FOREIGN LANGUAGES NEEDS OF SCOTTISH INDUSTRY AND COMMERCE: SURVEY REPORT

ALASTAIR DUNCAN
French Department
and
RICHARD JOHNSTONE
Education Department
University of Stirling

The study of how British firms use foreign languages has itself become a growth industry, sprouting from the LCCI Report of 1972 and the York Report of 1974 and coming to full flower in Steve Hagen's compilation of regional surveys, *Languages in British Business (1988)*.[1] From these various reports some broad conclusions have emerged. First, there is "a correlation between companies, commitment to language, and export success".[2] The BETRO Trust survey of 1979 found that 90% of language graduates employed in exporting within manufacturing companies were employed by winners of the Queen's award. Similarly, eight years later, the BOTB report *Into Active Exporting* reported that it was characteristic of active export firms to have staff and directors with some foreign language capability.[3]

Second, there is evidence in recent years of a shift in attitude towards foreign language use. More firms value foreign languages and more firms use them. The York Report of 1974 found that 70% of modern linguists believed that their companies had disregarded language skills when appointing them, and only 24.7% subsequently found their languages to be essential. By contrast, an Aston University survey of its graduates between 1976 and 1982 discovered that half needed to translate (though not employed as translators), two-thirds were writing letters and two-fifths needed interpreting skills[4] To some extent this trend to greater use may be due to the shift in the volume of Britain's trade away from traditional English-speaking markets to foreign-language ones. It remains remarkable, however, that between 1977 and 1984 Steve Hagen found a 10.6% increase in language use across matching samples of northern industry.[5]

Third, there are no grounds for complacency. Even the most positive of recent surveys find a patchy response. Broadly speaking one might say that the believers believe firmly: companies which have paid for language training are convinced thereafter that their investment was worthwhile.[6] There remain, however, many firms, among them successful exporters, who do not attach importance to language competence. Steve Hagen's 11 regional surveys, carried out between 1985-87, asked whether there were any countries in which firms could have significantly improved their trade performance over the last few years, given access to foreign language facilities. The answers ranged widely from 25% in the South East Region (where foreign languages are already most used) to 60% in Yorkshire. In only two regions was a 50% figure achieved.[7]

What then of Scotland? Until very recently little has been known about the Scottish scene. In 1985, Margaret Ross surveyed 160 manufacturing exporting firms in the West of Scotland. This was the single substantial study carried out before 1987/88.[8] It is particularly unfortunate that Scotland should have been relatively undersurveyed since Steve Hagen's studies have shown that use and needs vary from one area of the United Kingdom to another. Over the last twenty years, the Scottish economy has changed, broadly in line with that of the UK as a whole. It has shared in the massive shift in the pattern of trade away from the English-speaking markets of the ex-colonies to the European market, predominantly the EEC. It has seen a decline in heavy manufacturing industries, growth in new high technology industry and an overall switch of employment into the service sector. Like the rest of British industry, it faces the challenge of the Single European Market. On the other hand, the Scottish economy also has peculiarities which need to be taken into account. Within the service industries a special place is held by tourism, and the financial and insurance sectors. Within manufacturing industry, engineering remains very important, although the emphasis has switched in recent years from mechanical to electrical and instrument engineering, which together account for about one-third of manufacturing exports. Another major employer is the whisky industry accounting for about one-fifth of exports.[9] The top markets for Scottish manufactured goods (Table 1) show a distinctive pattern in which the countries of Western Europe are collectively more and more important, while both France and Germany have begun to rival the United States as the single most important export market. Lastly, the Scottish economy is served by an education system which is run and structured differently from that in the rest of the UK. If conclusions are to be drawn from surveys of business language need in Scotland, they must be implemented in terms of Standard Grade and Higher, of SCOTVEC modules and course descriptions, of courses run at FE colleges and Central Institutions.

Table 1: Top 15 markets for Scottish manufactured exports

Exports £m. (Rank)

Country	1987		1986		1985	
United States	884	(1)	898	(1)	1037	(1)
France	793	(2)	524	(2)	537	(3)
West Germany	770	(3)	481	(3)	698	(2)
Italy	559	(4)	307	(5)	373	(5)
Netherlands	319	(5)	380	(4)	416	(4)
Belgium	304	(6)	260	(6)	168	(7)
Switzerland	247	(7)	163	(9)	141	(10)
Spain	230	(8)	170	(7)	121	(12)
Sweden	210	(9)	115	(12)	153	(8)
Japan	182	(10)	167	(8)	193	(6)
Canada	161	(11)	126	(11)	127	(11)
Australia	130	(12)	146	(10)	150	(9)
Norway	117	(13)	99	(14)	100	(14)
Ireland	104	(14)	107	(13)	114	(13)
South Africa	70	(15)	56	(16)	54	(18)

Source: SCDI, 1988

The Stirling Survey: objectives and means

The Stirling University Survey of foreign language needs of Scottish industry was conceived early in 1988 with several objectives in mind:
- to establish which foreign language markets are perceived by Scottish firms to be most important, now and over the next few years
- to find out to what extent foreign languages are currently being used by firms in Scotland
- to discover what views firms take about their future need for foreign languages and the extent to which they are preparing themselves to meet that need
- to establish, as far as possible, how needs and attitudes vary from sector to sector
- to find out which categories of staff need languages and for what activities
- to discover what priority is being given to languages in the recruitment of staff and whether any shortages are or may become apparent
- to elicit business views of the language skills produced by the educational system and views of the language services provided by external agencies.

604 questionnaires were sent out in July 1988. 427 went to manufacturing firms, the remainder to firms and agencies in the service sector. The manufacturing firms were drawn from the Scottish Council for Development and Industry's list of exporting firms, 1988; the questionnaires were sent to a representative sample of small, medium and large firms within each of the SCDI's numbered classes, while an attempt was made to include the 100 top Scottish firms of 1987. The list of service firms was compiled from a number of sources. It was not known in advance which of these firms, in the service in manufacturing sectors, did business in non-English speaking markets.

In the event, 182 firms responded to the questionnaire, representing a return of approximately 31%. 176 were considered usable because they showed contacts with foreign language markets and some use of foreign languages. In a few cases, non-respondents wrote to explain why they were not responding. One firm explained that all matters relating to foreign countries were handled by their offices in England, another wrote that it was the firm's policy not to reply to questionnaires. The managing director of a well-known whisky firm wrote that he believed foreign languages were vital to the future of his sector, but that he had already spent thirty minutes on the questionnaire and could spare no more time on it. Table 2 shows the number of respondents broken down into types and sizes of firms.

Table 2: Respondents by type and size

Type and Size	Number of firms	% of total
Small manufacturing	83	47.2
Large manufacturing	32	18.2
Small service	29	16.4
Large service	32	18.2

small = 1-200 employees
large = over 200 employees

Commitment to non English speaking markets

Table 3 shows the percentage of firms currently exporting goods or services to non-English speaking markets, and their expectations of future trade.

**Table 3: Foreign language markets 1988; and expectations
1988-1993**

Language/trading area	% of respondents (N = 176)		
	current (Q3)	growth (Q4)	same (Q4)
French	49.7	53.1	12.3
German	47.5	46.9	15.6
Arabic	29.6	20.7	19.0
Italian	29.1	31.8	16.8
Spanish	26.2	30.1	13.4
Japanese	25.7	27.9	13.4
Russian	4.5	8.9	15.1
Other	32.4	17.9	4.5

In general, Table 3 reveals that the existing foreign-language markets are also the markets which are most expected to grow. This is the rule for markets in which French, German, Italian, Spanish and Japanese are the main languages. The only exception is the Arabic-speaking market which declines from third place as an existing market to sixth place as a market of potential growth. An insignificant percentage of respondents expected foreign-language markets to decline. But there were differences between the manufacturing and service sectors: the manufacturing sector was on the whole much more optimistic about growth. Small manufacturing firms give particular pride of place to Japan: 28 of the 83 small firms (34%) exported to Japan and the same number expected trade to grow. The comparable Japanese figures for the other sectors were: 5 large manufacturing (15.9%), 5 small service (17.5%) and 7 large service (21.8%).

A number of questions were asked to try to guage how committed firms were to the markets in which they were engaged. Two of the chosen indices involve direct contact with a foreign language: the production of foreign-language promotional material and subscription to a foreign-language trade journal. We also asked if firms employed an agent or distributor or had an associate company in a non English speaking country. If the indices are valid, then, as Table 4 shows, Germany pips

French-speaking countries as the trading area in which exporters are most active.

Table 4: Commitment to foreign language markets

Language/trading area   % of respondents (N = 176)

	agent/ distributor (Q7)	f-l promotional material (Q6)	sub to f-l trade journal (Q5)	associate company (Q8)
German	38.0	27.9	10.6	23.5
French	33.5	25.7	10.6	24.6
Italian	26.2	11.2	2.2	15.1
Japanese	22.3	12.3	1.7	10.6
Spanish	21.8	11.2	2.8	17.3
Arabic	16.8	5.6	1.1	14.0
Russian	4.5	3.9	0.6	2.3
Other	19.6	13.4	3.4	16.2

Italy comes relatively high for the employment of agents and there is a remarkable amount of promotional material in Japanese. (Who reads over it to check it?) Small manufacturers were almost as active in using agents and distributors as large manufacturers; but large manufacturers produce much more promotional material: 83 small manufacturers produced 69 items, while 32 large manufacturers produced 83. But in the case of Japanese, the ratio was more than reversed: 8 small manufacturers produced Japanese literature compared to 2 large manufacturers. The 32 large service companies took 19 journals between them, more than any other group.

Current use of English and foreign languages

Table 5: Use of English v foreign language: % of respondents (N 176)

Language/ trading area	English	Transactions (Q12)		f-l	f-l mail (Q9)		Replies to f-l letters(Q11)	
		both Eng. & f-l	f-l	sent to agency	handled in firm	in English	in f-l	

	English	both Eng. & f-l	f-l	sent to agency	handled in firm	in English	in f-l
French	55.3	19.6	7.3	15.0	58.6	52.0	26.8
German	60.3	11.2	5.0	19.5	46.4	51.4	21.2
Spanish	46.4	6.1	2.2	21.2	21.8	45.2	12.9
Italian	45.2	3.9	1.7	19.5	20.7	38.7	11.2
Japanese	43.0	2.8	0.6	22.3	2.8	40.8	5.0
Arabic	40.8	1.1	1.7	22.9	2.2	39.7	3.3
Russian	26.8	1.7	0.0	18.9	2.8	31.7	3.3

Three questions were asked to find out how much firms use foreign languages. The first three columns in Table 5 give a very general answer. They show that in dealings with foreign-language companies, English is by far the predominant language. These figures largely correspond to Margaret Ross's findings. To express the figures in her terms: of all transactions with the USSR, 94.1% are in English (Ross: 90%). The totals for other languages are: Arabic, 93.6% in English (Ross 94%); Japanese, 92.7% (Ross 95%); Italian, 89% (Ross 81%); Spanish, 84.9% (Ross 68%); German, 78.9% (Ross 82%); French, 67.3% (Ross 68%).[10] But when one looks at the last four columns of Table 5, a much more complex picture of language use emerges. How do firms deal with a letter, fax or telex written in a foreign language (columns 4 and 5)? In the cases of French and German, a very significant majority of such communications are read and actioned within the firm; and about half of all communications in Spanish and Italian are dealt with in the same way. When it comes to replying to foreign-language letters (columns 6 and 7), the amount of use falls back sharply. Even so, more than a quarter of firms receiving letters in Italian claim to reply in that language. And the figures for French, German and Spanish are higher. It is not clear whether these replies are written within the firms or by an external agency; at the very least they imply a company policy on foreign-language letters.

All in all then, Table 5 suggests that foreign languages are more used than some previous surveys have shown, although that use may be occasional. The contrast in use between transactions and letter-reading may reflect both necessity and the skills learned in school. Faced with a letter in French, some employee of the firm will dredge up sufficient school French to get the gist of it. Faced with a live Frenchman, the firms resort to English. In other words, the Scottish businessman or woman, in so far as he or she commands a foreign language at all, can read but cannot, or prefers not to, speak. Yet this hypothesis still does not explain how 46.4% of firms read mail in German, 21.8% in Spanish, and 20.7% in Italian. The Scottish education system certainly did not prepare future managers, sales personnel or secretaries to undertake these tasks. They must have learned the languages, especially German, since leaving school. This evidence of the current use of languages supports the case for diversification of language teaching in schools. That case is strengthened when one looks at future need.

Future needs and policy

Of 176 firms responding to the questionnaire, 123 indicated that their need for foreign languages would grow over the next one to five years. Table 6 shows the breakdown by languages.

Table 6: Future need of languages 1988-93

| Language/ | % of respondents (Q13) | | |
trading area	more need	same need	less need
French	60.3	22.9	0.6
German	53.6	21.2	1.1
Italian	38.0	16.2	0.6
Spanish	36.3	17.3	0.6
Japanese	22.9	18.4	1.1
Arabic	14.0	19.6	1.7
Russian	10.6	14.5	1.7
Other	7.8	5.0	1.1

Small services firms showed a particularly strong interest in French, German and Spanish. More than a quarter of small manufacturers expressed a need for Japanese - which tallies with the projected growth in exports to Japan envisaged by small manufacturers (34%).

Table 7 shows the responses to two supplementary questions which asked whether a better command of a foreign language or greater knowledge of social and business practice and protocol could, in certain language areas, significantly benefit the firm. The first question closely parallels an item in Steve Hagen's questionnaire and, for comparison, Table 7 includes Hagen's UK average response."

Table 7: Firms underperforming for lack of languages or of social and business protocol

Languages trading area	a. languages (Q18) % of respondents		b. social and business protocol(Q19) % of respondents
	Scotland 1988	UK average 1985-87	Scotland 1988
French	49.7	23	30.1
German	45.8	19	27.4
Italian	25.1	9	15.1
Spanish	21.8	13	15.6
Japanese	19.6	6	25.1
Arabic	10.6	10	6.1
Russian	6.7	4	6.1

Several points arise from Table 7. First, the rank order of demand is not the same throughout the UK. German and French come fairly consistently at the top of Hagen's surveys; Spanish often follows them. But in Scotland Italian and Japanese come particularly high on the list. Second, the Stirling University survey, both overall and in relation to particular languages, shows a considerably greater demand for languages than was found in any region in Hagen's survey. This may be partly to do with the phrasing of the question: Hagen asked about benefits in the "last few years" rather than in the present or the future. But the difference may have much more to do with a new perception of language need following the first round of government publicity about the challenge of 1992.

A further question in the Stirling survey asked specifically whether firms were adopting a languages policy in preparation for 1992. 67 firms (38%) answered in the affirmative. Table 8 correlates the number of firms which saw a growing need for languages with the number which were adopting - or not adopting - a policy on languages.

Table 8: Future language needs and policy

No. of languages required by firms with growing needs (Q13)	no. of respondents with policy (Q30)	without policy (Q30)
1	7	5
2	13	18
3	14	11
4	14	13
5	10	4
6	4	1
7	4	2
8	1	2
	67	56

Overall, Table 8 shows that just over half of the firms which perceived an increased need for languages thought that a policy was necessary to fulfil that need. One can only salute the courage of the two firms which foresee an increased need in eight foreign languages but which do not intend to adopt a policy. 65 firms added a comment on the topic of language policy. The small number of negative comments mainly indicated that the firms would rely on English. The positive comments showed that in many cases, the policy was an intention not yet clearly focussed. Recruitment of new foreign-language speaking staff was spoken of more than the exploitation or development of existing skills, although a number of comments acknowledged the importance both of motivation and of training: "We shall bring staff into contact with foreign-language transactions, highlighting to them the need for foreign languages and the benefits of linguistic skills, and so encourage them to find a way of improving their skills".

Language need in specific sectors

Given the structure of the Scottish economy, it would be particularly useful to have an accurate assessment of language need in specific areas, for example electrical and instrument engineering, the whisky industry or the tourist trade. Unfortunately, in the present survey the number of responses for any particular industrial class was not large enough to permit statistically reliable conclusions to be drawn. (Table 14 and 15, at Appendix 1, show the full breakdown of responses by industrial class). Nevertheless, some largely impressionistic conclusions suggest themselves.

A low response rate was sometimes associated with a low evaluation of languages need among the few firms which responded. This was the case with **non-metallic products**: the only two out of sixteen firms to reply foresaw little increased need for languages over the next five years. In other classes, it seemed that the survey had attracted responses from a minority of enthusiasts: in the case of **printing, paper and publishing** only six of nineteen questionnaires were returned; five of the firms saw an increased need for a range of languages and the same five had language policies; all five firms were in paper rather than in printing and publishing. The highest response rate from any one class came from the **insurance** sector, with six replies to nine questionnaires. A very small proportion of the business of all six companies was done with non English-speaking countries, and only two expected expansion in this area. Yet four thought their language needs would grow and three were in the process of devising language policies.

Table 9 summarises the responses of some of the larger samples from industrial classes which play an important part in the Scottish economy. Large in this context means classes for which at leart thirty questionnaires were sent out or at least ten returned. The figures in Table 9 are not percentages but show the actual number of firms which responded in general and to particular questions.

Table 9: Language need in specific classes of industry

Class	Question-naires		Future Exports (Q4)			lang need (Q13)			lang policy (Q30)
	sent	rec'd	more	same	less	more	same	less	
Mechanical engineering	58	18	6	7	-	7	8	1	3
Electronics, electrical & instrument engineering	42	16	13	3	-	13	2	-	5
Food & drink	51	9	6	1	-	8	-	-	6
Textiles	66	23	23	-	-	16	7	-	11
Travel & tourism	23	9	5	1	-	6	3	-	5

Mechanical engineering: just above the average response rate of 30%; fairly evenly divided as to whether exports and languages need would grow or stay the same.

Electronics and electrical engineering: appended comments and replies to specific questions suggested that almost all **written** communications were in English, "or in American actually" : "occasionally we translate the odd sentence into the recipient's language, just to show willing!" Nevertheless, ten of the thirteen respondents foresee an increased need for French, eight for German and three for all the languages specified in the questionnaire. The activities in which greater need was forecast involved in the main listening and speaking (e.g. in travelling abroad or using the phone) and reading (e.g. letters, fax, technical and sales literature). Seven firms, just over half the sample, wanted the education system to produce more managerial, secretarial, professional and scientific staff competent in a foreign language. In the subclass of **instrument engineering**, three of the total samples of four firms returned the questionnaire. Two of the three had language policies for 1992. All three mentioned several languages and saw an increased need for French, German and Spanish.

Food and drink: very poor response rate; but a high proportion of respondents had a policy and see need for more language use (seven for French, four for German, six for Spanish). The whisky industry was poorly represented in replies to the questionnaire.

Textiles: above average response rate; main need for French, German, Spanish, Italian which, with Japan, are seen as main future export areas. A high proportion of respondents commented positively, e.g.: "It is our policy to use foreign languages wherever possible in transactions with our customers. Those staff who already speak languages are encouraged to use them regularly in the field, on the telephone and in correspondence. If they wish to learn further languages, this is encouraged and paid for. We would also ultimately look to recruit further staff with languages ability."

Travel and tourism: above average rate of response. Four respondents were hotel chains, which were evenly divided on the need for a language policy. Two transport companies foresaw a slightly increased need for French and German. An association for the preservation of Scotland's heritage gave a cautiously positive response, while pointing out that only 4% of visitors to its properties and 0.5% of its total income came from non-English-speaking areas. The most positive plans and policies came from the Department of Public Relations and Tourism of a large local authority and from the Scottish Tourist Board.

What are foreign languages used for, and by whom?

Table 10: Principal activities, current and predicted 1988-93

% of respondents

Activity	current use	future use		
		more	same	less
Reading letters, telex, fax	52.5	52.0	19.0	1.7
Discussion, eg buying, selling, negotiating	46.9	50.2	16.8	1.7
Travelling abroad	41.9	49.6	17.3	2.8
Using the phone	39.7	44.7	17.3	2.8
Writing letters	26.2	42.4	12.3	1.7
Entertaining and socialising	27.9	33.5	25.1	2.2
Reading technical/sales texts	19.0	29.1	15.1	2.2
Writing trade documents	10.6	18.4	14.0	2.2
Listening to talks	5.0	17.3	17.9	1.7
Writing technical manuals	6.1	15.6	15.6	2.2
Giving talks and speeches	4.5	14.5	16.2	2.8
Drafting legal agreements	7.2	14.5	32.4	2.2

The figures in the first column in Table 10 correspond closely to the findings of previous UK surveys: reading comes top of the list, followed by three activities which primarily involve listening and speaking; then comes writing. Previous surveys, however, have not always included the activity described here as "discussion e.g. buying, selling, negotiating". The second top place of this activity clearly expresses a need for high-level oral skills. Indeed, the large manufacturers put this skill top of the list, while the small service also gave priority to oral skills by giving joint first place to travel abroad and using the phone. The same priorities appear in exactly the same order in the projection of future needs (column 2). While the main demand is for general skills, it is noteworthy that firms foresee a doubling in the limited need for such specialist skills as writing technical manuals or drafting legal agreements.

Table 11: Users of foreign languages: current and predicted (1988-1993)

Categories of personnel	% of respondents			
	current	more	same	less
Managerial/Executive	54.7	56.4	22.4	0.6
Sales	39.7	47.0	15.1	0.6
Advertising/Marketing	22.3	34.6	13.4	0.6
Secretarial/Receptionist	15.6	22.2	19.0	0.6
Production	7.8	10.6	20.7	0.6
Research	6.7	10.6	19.6	0.0
Finance	6.2	8.9	21.8	6.0
Design	5.6	11.2	20.7	0.0
Purchasing	5.6	10.6	20.7	1.1
Tranport/Distribution	5.6	12.3	20.7	0.0
Contracts	4.5	14.5	16.2	0.0
Accounts	4.0	9.5	21.8	1.1

Table 11 confirms previous surveys that the main language needs, current and predicted, are for decision-makers and negotiators with an important subsidiary need for secretarial staff. The small manufacturers put managerial staff top of their list, as did the service firms; the large manufacturers gave highest priority to sales staff. There was some perception of a greater language need for transport/distribution personnel and staff responsible for contracts and for design. The low perception of need for research staff could indicate, regrettably, how little research work is carried on in Scotland.

Recruitment

22.9% of firms responding to the survey had taken on a Modern Languages graduate within the last three years; within the same period 24.6% of firms had explicitly used "command of a foreign language" as one criterion when advertising for a new employee. Firms who had thus stipulated foreign language competence required, in descending rank order: sales staff (52.3%), managerial/executive (43.1%), secretarial/receptionist (25.0%), advertising/marketing (20.5%) and contracts (11.4%). The languages in demand were: French (81.8%), German (63.6%), Spanish (34.1%), Italian (25.0%), Japanese (9.1%), Arabic (9.1%) and Russian (6.8%). A few firms had also looked for speakers of Portugese and Dutch. Both the choice of personnel and the range of languages confirms the patterns of need which emerge elsewhere in the survey. In view of the relatively low demand for speakers of foreign languages, it was disquieting to find that a fairly significant proportion of firms had failed to recruit suitably qualified candidates, even when French was required. In the case of other languages, the situation was worse. The explanation may be that candidates could not be found who combined professional expertise with additional competence in a foreign language.

Table 12: Recruits wanted and not found by 176 firms, 1985-88
(Q23)

Language	no. of recruits	no. not found	% not found
French	37	5	13.5
German	31	6	19.3
Spanish	14	4	28.5
Japanese	4	3	75.0
Dutch	2	2	100.0

(For each of the following languages one recruit was wanted and found: Swedish, Danish, Chinese, Serbo-croat and Turkish)

Views on education

In view of firms' failure to recruit qualified foreign language speakers, it was not surprising to find mixed perceptions of the educational system.

One third of respondents believed that schools, colleges and universities are producing people with the right skills to satisfy their foreign language needs. Of those who had recruited foreign language graduates, the vast majority were satisfied with them, and appeared to value their foreign language skills. Asked to comment on the nature of the benefits brought to the firms by these recruits, most firms placed first (80.5%) their general ability to communicate and second (73%) their command of a foreign language. Their knowledge of foreign countries was valued much less highly (34.1%).

Another third of respondents were neutral or chose not to comment on education. The final third, however, were not satisfied with its products. The main demand of such firms was that potential employees in all fields should, in addition, be trained in a foreign language. 46% of firms wanted more graduates in business and management with foreign language skills, 44% wanted more secretarial staff, 28% more professional, research, technical and scientific staff. There was an allied demand from 35% of firms that foreign language teaching should be more fully integrated with the teaching of technical and commercial subjects.

These criticisms may be thought to point in two directions: at business, technical and professional courses which leave no space or time for language acquisition; at university courses which do not incorporate a vocational element. A number of appended comments, however, placed the problem elsewhere: "It is not tertiary education's job to teach basic languages - a graduate has enough on his plate getting a degree in his discipline without doing a language as well! Everybody should do at least one language in primary school and all but the least able should be able to converse in two or more by the end of secondary school".

Use of external agencies

Over half (58%) of respondents had used an interpreting or translating agency in the last three years (this is near the UK average of 60%, as established by Hagen, 1988); only 17% had used a language school. It is clear that most firms tend to buy in languages help rather than train their personnel to answer their language needs. The more frequent and pressing such needs become, the more expensive becomes this manner of meeting them.

Around 20% of firms use translating or interpreting agencies for Spanish, German, Italian, Japanese, Arabic and Russian; 15% for French, as shown above in Table 5. Almost unanimously (95%), respondents declared themselves fairly or very satisfied with the service they received. Of those who expressed any measure of dissatisfaction, seven firms wanted greater accuracy, and only three required a faster service. This degree of satisfaction is perhaps not entirely compatible with the findings of Table 13: too high a percentage of letters in the rarer languages take too long to become available in English.

Table 13: Time taken to translate foreign-language mail (Q10)

Language	% of respondents		
	up to 24 hrs	2-3 days	7 days or more
French	69.3	9.5	1.1
German	60.9	12.3	1.1
Spanish	36.9	16.2	2.2
Italian	35.7	14.5	1.1
Japanese	14.0	13.4	5.6
Arabic	12.3	15.1	5.6
Russian	12.3	8.9	6.7
Other	7.3	5.0	-

Of the 29 firms who had dealt with a language school, 22 were very or fairly satisfied. Eight firms would like to see language schools offering a wider range of languages and only eight reported that they had run on-site language courses. As far as we are aware, no company in Scotland has its own in-house language trainers.

General conclusions

A clear majority of the firms surveyed perceive an increased need for foreign languages over the next 1-5 years. Two languages of Western Europe (French and German), followed by two other languages of Western Europe (Spanish and Italian), followed by Japanese, are well ahead of all others. In many cases, firms perceive a need for more than one foreign language. Opinions based on personal anecdotal evidence that we live in an increasingly anglophone world have been shown by our findings to be invalid. Many of those responsible for running Scottish industry clearly take the view that foreign-language competence will be important to them, and they are looking to the educational sector to help provide this.

Previous surveys may have underestimated foreign language use; in particular, we have found that many firms make a considerable effort to read incoming foreign-language mail. In any event, there are clear signs of a more positive attitude towards foreign languages among top personnel. Although Margaret Ross put a brave face on things by urging providers of language courses to go out and conquer an unexploited market, she found little to suggest that Scottish firms valued or wished to improve their foreign language skills.[12] The present survey shows that many firms now do want their employees to command a wider range of languages and that a considerable proportion intend to adopt a policy to achieve this end.

No doubt, this more positive attitude towards foreign languages reflects a changed climate. The Single European Market has concentrated the minds of the business community on many future challenges, including the need for foreign languages. The CBI in Scotland has become a forceful advocate of a new attitude; in May 1988 John Davidson, its Director, summarised the case for languages in a striking phrase: "English is no longer the international language of business. Today's international language of business is the native language of the customer". During 1987-88, preparations were underway for the establishment of a Scottish Language Export Centre. These preparations included a sample survey of the language needs of Scottish business. Other surveys were carried out in 1988: by the Scottish Association for Language Teaching (on the tourist industry), by Grampian Regional Council (on local industry) and by CILT, as part of a UK study of tourist-related industries.[13] The Stirling University survey has provided statistical evidence to show that all this activity has begun to bear fruit: the message is getting through.

Implications for industry, commerce and education

Some firms have language policies, but at the moment these tend to be vague. The educational sector can play a useful role, not only in helping personnel in firms to extend their competence in foreign languages, but also to refine their thinking on what their foreign-language needs are and on how they might best be met. The conventional view of foreign-language learning held by many schoolteachers was that it took at least five years before a valid level of competence in (largely written) communication could be attained by only a small elite. It is possible that some business people still hold to that view, and that, in consequence, they see foreign-language competence as too remote a goal for themselves and their staff. Those involved in the educational sector, as a result of ten years of research and development, have learnt that valid and perfectly usable levels of communication may be developed by learners of all aptitudes within a much shorter time-scale; and in consequence they may be in a position to help those in the business sector to understnd that command of foreign languages may be an asset to them that is not only potentially useful to some but also in practice attainable by many.

By the early 1990's, Scottish firms will be employing young people of all aptitudes (including school leavers at age 16) who, as a result of recent government policy, will have developed a basic competence in communication in at least one foreign language allied to a substantial awareness of at least one foreign way of life, since they will have taken at least one foreign language throughout the first four years of secondary school. This will constitute a valuable resource for industry and commerce in Scotland. At present there is, understandably, little evidence that firms are aware of this potential resource (the survey was conducted only one month after the announcement of the Secretary of State's policy statement on foreign languages in schools). In consequence, it will be essential to develop a means of communication between industry and education in Scotland to plan how this resource by be extended and exploited.

Implication for foreign language provision in Scottish education

The survey findings offer considerable encouragement to those responsible for developing Standard Grade and Higher, since the combinations of skills required by Scottish business firms (mainly, various combinations of listening, speaking and reading, but also with more specific kinds of writing) are essentially the same as those developed through the Standard Grade and Higher syllabuses. Furthermore, the importance to firms of discussion in a foreign language, clearly indicates that a genuine level of competence is required, and not a collection of tourist phrases.

The findings also indicate a need to encourage greatly increased numbers of school pupils to carry on with a foreign language beyond Standard Grade. The categories of business personnel who, at present, are considered most likely to require foreign-language competence are in management and sales. Mention must also be made of the potential foreign-language needs of the professions of engineering, accountancy and law. Students at school are likely to increase their chances of employment, of advancement and of variety of work experience after 1992 if they stay on at school and indeed beyond school, in order to obtain the highest possible qualifications, while continuing their foreign-language study. Within the business sector, those who can speak Japanese should find themselves in particular demand. But the most immediate and pressing need is for more teachers at all levels, on whom will fall the responsibility of producing this new generation of competent foreign-language speakers.

Finally, there is an obvious mismatch between the output of the education system and the requirements of industry and commerce. Of course, the aim of teaching foreign languages in school, college or university is not, and should not, be solely to meet the requirements of business. Nor need there be a perfect match between the range of languages offered within the school system and the range required by business firms. But at present most Scottish university courses remain primarily of a literary type; many commercial and technical Higher National Diploma courses exclude foreign languages; and what school pupils mainly learn is French. Changes are required if business need is even partially to be met. No change is more urgently required than that of diversifying language provision: more pupils must learn German, Italian and Spanish; and somewhere in the educational system there must be more opportunity to learn Japanese.

November 1988

APPENDIX

Table 14: Questionnaires sent and returned: manufacturing sector

Questionnaires

Manufacturing class

	sent	recd	% response
Metal Manufacturers	12	3	25.0
Non-metallic mineral products	16	2	12.5
Chemical producers	22	7	31.8
Finished metal products	22	6	27.2
Mech. engineering	59	18	31.0
Electronic and electrical engineering	42	13	30.9
Motor industry	9	3	33.0
Instrument engineering	4	3	75.0
Food and drink	53	9	17.0
Textile	68	23	33.8
Footwear and leather	34	10	29.4
Timber and furniture	11	2	18.1
Paper, printing and publishing	21	6	28.5
Rubber and plastic	15	5	33.0
Misc. industries	25	5	20.0

Table 15: Questionnaires sent and returned: service sector

Service class	Questionnaires		
	sent	recd	% response
Travel and tourism	23	9	39.1
Banks	13	3	23.0
Insurance companies	9	6	66.0
Corporate finance	11	2	18.0
Invest, trust and stock market	9	4	44.4
Chartered accountants	13	8	61.5
Corporate lawyers	15	2	13.3
Marketing and advertising	11	5	45.5
Large miscellaneous*	43	12	27.9
Transport and haulage	8	1	12.5
Import and export	5	2	40.0
Shipping companies and agents	13	3	23.1
Misc. services	12	4	33.3

* composed largely of firms from list of top 100 firms in Scotland in 1987, eg builders, holding companies, etc.

Acknowledgements

This survey was funded by the Scottish Education Department and by the Scottish Development Agency. The authors wish to express their thanks to the research assistants who worked on it, Grace Swayne and Lene Langlands.

Notes

1. *The Non-specialist Use of Foreign Languages in Industry and Commerce*, London Chamber of Commerce and Industry Examinations Board, 1972, revised 1985; K. Emmans, E. Hawkins, and A. Westoby, *Foreign Languages in Industry and Commerce*, Language Teaching Centre, University of York, 1974; S. Hagen (ed), *Languages in British Business. An Analysis of Current Needs*, CILT/Newcastle upon Tyne Polytechnic, 1988.

2. Hagen, 1988, p. xviii.

3. *A Study of Languages and Export Performance*, the Royal Society of Arts/Betro Trust, 1979, pp. 13-16; *Into Active Exporting*, BOTB, 1987, p. 13.

4. Cited in D. Liston, and N. Reeves, *Business Studies, Languages and Overseas Trade: A Study of Education and Training*, Macdonald and Evans/Institute of Export, 1985, p. 118.

5. Hagen, 1988, p. xix.

6. Liston and Reeves, 1985, pp. 118-119.

7. Hagen, 1988, p. xxii

8. *The Language Needs of Firms in the West of Scotland*, in Hagen, 1988, pp. 65-73.

9. *Scotland: an Economic Profile*, Scottish Office, 1988, pp. 20-21, 29-32.

10. Ross in Hagen, 1988, p. 69.

11. Hagen, 1988, p. xxii.

12. Ross in Hagen, 1988, p. 72.

13. *Language Skills in the Tourist Industry in Scotland*, Scottish Association for Language Teaching, 1988; *An Investigation into Foreign Language Usage in Grampian Industry and the Implications for the Curriculum*, Grampian Regional Council, 1988; *Use and Availability of Foreign-Language Skills in Tourist-related Industries in Britain*, CILT, on behalf of the British Tourist Authority, 1987-88.

A EUROPEAN PERSPECTIVE

H.R. McMAHON
Member of the European Parliament
Strathclyde West

There are two irreconcilable facts which point to the absolute necessity of European Community action on the teaching of modern languages. The first of these is the recent Eurobarometer survey which revealed that one out of two people in Europe considers his or her knowledge of a foreign language insufficient to participate in a conversation. The second inescapable reality is that in 1992 and beyond, the accessibility of Europe, in terms of business, education, culture and media, will affect us all and will of necessity alter our present horizons. The incompatibility of these situations will soon become apparent, and the seriousness of the results will drive home our predicament.

The advent of the Internal Market, and sheer hard-headed business sense is only one aspect of the whole picture. The facilitation of the free movement of persons, heralded by the recent agreement in Europe of the mutual recognition of professional qualifications, is another. Linguistic testing will form part of this system, which in the present situation could lead only to an unfair shift in the balance of practising professions, with the UK attracting foreign nationals without the possibility of a reciprocal exodus of British professional people - because they cannot speak the language. In a recent article on the differences between foreign language provision in Scottish schools and the provision in continental European Community countries, Peter Wheeldon pointed out that in most EC countries a foreign language is compulsorily studied for seven or eight years, in Scotland for only two.[1] This situation creates, clearly, an unevenness of availability which will detrimentally affect the right of consumers within the Community. Those who do not have access to language opportunities will immediately be at a disadvantage. The European Community must not reinforce this discrimination.

On a broader level, the cultural richness which language learning brings is widely recognised at European level, and the need to foster this has been restated time and again. The mutual understanding which arises from the study of our neighbours' languages is worth a thousand trade and defence agreements at government level - a fact already recognised by France and West Germany in their mutual attempts at linguistic repricicocity. The needs and benefits are, therefore, clear, and need not, at this Conference, especially be elaborated upon. We are all agreed that the requirements are paramount; how can these needs best be satisfied?

EEC Initiatives

Both the European Parliament and the Commission have a good record in taking initiatives on modern languages.

In 1984, the Council of Ministers and Ministers of Education agreed to promote practical knowledge of two languages in addition to the mother tongue. A European Parliament Report of 1985 called for Member States to take into consideration the conclusions of a Council of Ministers meeting of 3 June 1985 which concentrated on providing specific aid for language teaching in the "peripheral" regions, especially Ireland, Greece, Portugal and Scotland, where it is more difficult for the children to come into contact with people speaking a different language.

The European Parliament has also been responsible for many resolutions on the subject of Modern Language teaching, and the Committee on Youth Culture, Education, Information and Sports, of which I am a member, regularly introduces initiatives on the subject. In October 1988, a Report on the Teaching of Modern Languages was almost unanimously approved in Strasbourg. Between 1984 and 1985, the Commission awarded one hundred or so short study grants for bilingual specialists to study other European systems of linguistic education. In this context, the example of the West German system of bilingual education was examined and its possibilities of application in this country were studied.

By facilitating the exchange of students and young people, the ERASMUS, COMETT and YES Programmes[2] have fostered cultural, industrial and linguistic links among the Member States of the EEC. The establishment of the Eurydice Network has also been a vital component in linguistic exchanges. On a more general, cultural level, European Parliament resolutions have included suggestions that the media could also be involved by broadcasting films, documentaries and so on in their original languages to foster at least passive knowledge of foreign languages.

In addition, the Community will be seeking to promote exchanges of information and experience in approaches to language learning. The conclusions of the 1984 Council of Ministers provided the idea of the possibility of conferences at Community level, or at Member State level, organised along similar lines to the one at Stirling University and involving all interested parties. Ideas and methods would then be exchanged on a formal basis. This organised means of contact could have many consequences, not least of which would be the possibility of the establishment of a Europe-wide Consultative Committee of Experts to oversee professional training standards and to supervise Member States' activities in this field. Such a co-ordination of effort could also be a sound basis for better co-operation between Member States in language teaching and in the training of teachers. This suggestion was reiterated in a European Parliament Resolution of 11th November, 1986, which called for the funding of more research into teaching methods and in the training of teachers. Dissemination of the results of such efforts could then be achieved at a Community level, and savings could be made on the duplication of research.

LINGUA

Using the existing framework as a base, therefore, the European Commission, in January of 1989, put forward a proposal entitled LINGUA which is intended to further promote the training, teaching and learning of foreign languages in Europe. LINGUA involves the diversification of foreign languages rather than the promotion of one or two priority languages, and sees as paramount an improvement in the quality and quantity of foreign language teachers and trainers. One of the main thrusts of LINGUA is also in the vocational training field. The LINGUA proposal was approved in modified form by the Council of Ministers in May 1989.

The first phase of the programme is planned to run from 1990-1994. The overall budget for the first five years of the programme will be 130 million pounds. LINGUA will consist of three main elements. The first of these will be inter-university co-operation programmes, with an annual financial ceiling of 25,000 Ecu per institution. The second element is the provision of students grants, direct financial support from the Commission, with a basic minimum of 150 grants to each Member State. The grants will be awarded and administered through ERASMUS.

Grants will also be made available for the mobility and exchange of teachers and trainers, which would enable them to plan and prepare inter-university co-operation programmes with parties in other Member States, and to exchange experience on the latest developments. In the field of initial training the Community can, by awarding grants or by other means, as LINGUA proposes, encourage all future language teachers to complete their training by spending a period of vocational preparation in the country whose language they intend to teach. In in-service training, the Community intends to provide a certain number of teachers with an opportunity to spend a vocational and cultural "refresher" period in the country whose language they teach, by means of exchanges between teachers, trainee periods, study visits or seminars.

The third element concerns economic life. Here the Community will provide support for the development and dissemination of "foreign language 1992 audits" designed to enable enterprises, particularly small and medium-sized enterprises, to specify the extent of their foreign language needs and training requirements. The Community will also provide support on a pilot basis for the development of specific foreign language training materials for different sectors of economic life, e.g.

commercial and legal sectors. An exchange scheme will be set up for representatives of small and medium-sized enterprises, and for those involved in language training in economic life. Potential linkages with the DELTA, MEDIA and COMETT programmes are also evisaged in this field.

An advisory committee is to be set up to aid the Commission in the scheme. Two representatives are to be drawn from each Member State, appointed by the Commission on the basis of proposals from the Member States concerned.

The LINGUA proposals invite Members States to designate a national centre specialising in the field of foreign language teaching developments so as to exchange ideas and information on a continuing basis. The Commission was invited to arrange the necessary co-ordination and co-operation between these centres, drawing on the experience and contacts of the existing EURYDICE network in the European Community.

Conclusion

The Scottish Office proposal that all pupils should continue to study one foreign language throughout the four compulsory years of secondary school is very much to be welcomed - even if it falls short of the Commission's original proposal to make two languages compulsory for every pupil. The funding and teaching of the new language proposals remains problematic. But it is clear, despite previous disappointments at Member State level, that we now have a new awareness of the importance of language teaching as an element of basic education. Initiatives from the European Parliament, the new LINGUA programme, and the new policy for Scottish schools open up fresh possibilities for the teaching of modern languages in a European context.

November 1988/May 1989

Notes

1. P. Wheeldon, "Scotland and Europe - a comparative study of opportunities in foreign language learning in schools", *Modern Languages in Scotland*, University of Strathclyde/Scottish Society of the Institute of Linguists, 1988, pp. 23-29 (p.24)

2. An explanation of these acronyms is given in the Glossary at the end of this volume.

CONCLUSION: THE WAY AHEAD

ALASTAIR DUNCAN and RICHARD JOHNSTONE

Why do we in Scotland need foreign languages as we move towards the last decade of the 20th century? Ann Carnachan, Anne Lorne Gillies and Hugh McMahon have spelt out reasons which have to do with our development as indviduals. Learning a language can help pupils to appreciate how language works and to develop the skills necessary for successful communication. Language also has to do with our sense of identity: we are formed by what we speak. Learning another language, especially in combination with some study of another culture, can open our eyes to new perspectives on the world and so enrich the way we see ourselves. The earlier we are exposed to cultural differences, the more chance there is that we shall develop tolerance and understanding for what seems initially foreign: a German tourist, Dad or Mum's Japanese boss, the girl or boy in the class who is both Scottish and Pakistani. All this, together with the flexibility of young minds and tongues, forms the essence of the argument for teaching languages in Primary schools.

In the 1990's and beyond there will be more and more contact between the countries and peoples of the European Community. Progressively, qualifications will be mutually recognised and work permits will become redundant. Hugh McMahon has pointed out how unfortunate it will be if our fellow Europeans can find jobs in Scotland, but our own citizens cannot work on the Continent because they cannot speak a foreign language. What chance will a young person from Scotland have in competing for a job in a European company against a contemporary from Holland, if the Scot speaks only English while the Dutchman or woman with the same qualifications speaks their own language and two or three others besides? It is not only the top jobs in management, the professions and the civil service which are at stake. One example: up to the present each member state of the EEC has been granted a fixed quota of permits for lorry drivers on long haul international routes. Post-1992 these quota arrangements will lapse. The French have already seen the opportunities this will create for their road haulage industry and have embarked on an extensive English language training programme designed specifically for that industry, from managing directors to drivers. If we fail to prepare our current and future lorry drivers for Europe after 1992, both they and the haulage industry will suffer. All this forms the core of the case for teaching foreign languages to all, and not just the smattering of a language but a working knowledge, which means differing levels of competence for different jobs and individuals.

In his opening statement, the Minister of State forcefully reiterates the economic arguments for learning foreign languages at a time when more than 50% of our trade is now with the countries of Western Europe. Sir Gerald Elliot stresses the need to have foreign-language users at different levels within firms, at the levels of operation, management and policy. Ann Ryley demonstrates in telling detail the benefits which her firm derives from its use of languages: "Speaking the customer's language is the only way not to be totally dependent on your agents". The Stirling survey has shown that many Scottish firms are now convinced that they need languages if they are to prosper in the challenging climate of the Single European market. French and German come joint top of the list, with Italian and Spanish in equal third place. That diversification could be justified on cultural as well as business grounds greatly enhances the argument for diversification of language provision in schools.

The Secretary of State's circular of July 1988 recognised the benefit of foreign language education and set out new guidelines to improve the provision of language teaching in Scotland. In May 1989 the Council of Ministers of the EEC approved the LINGUA programme, albeit in modified form, releasing 130 million pounds to improve language training in the European Community over the next five years. What are the implications of these developments and what now requires most urgently to be done?

First, it is apparent both from the Stirling survey of business needs and from the papers by Ian Lockerbie and Harry Dresner that there continues to be a gap between education and industry. While many firms recognise they have a growing need for foreign languages, they are vague as to how they can best satisfy that need. Clearer policies are needed on the recruitment of foreign language speakers, on the training and re-training of staff in foreign languages and on the exploitation of foreign languages especially in the conquest of new markets. Meanwhile, foreign language study in the universities is undergoing a transformation which is far from complete. Although communicative language teaching has made much ground, the relative importance of area studies and literary studies remains a delicate issue. One healthy sign is the proliferation of new degree programmes which combine a foreign language not just with business studies, but with disciplines such as economics, law, medicine and engineering. By contrast, it is disquieting to learn from Harry Dresner that languages are not given adequate teaching time in many scientific and technical degree and SCOTVEC programmes and that in the creation of some new degree schemes languages have been squeezed out altogether. We can only reiterate his plea that an "unequivocal" sign is needed from the SED that space must be made "to provide full language options integral to course structures and earning realistic study credits".

LINGUA may help to bridge the gap between education and industry, but it will be important to ensure that the application of the programme in Scotland is given a distinctive Scottish dimension. That implies consultation between education and business in Scotland to establish priorities, and full recognition from Brussels of the distinctive nature of the education and teacher training system, in Scotland. Funding should be administered from Scotland rather than from London.

The picture for the future in schools is one of opportunities that appear almost dazzling, when compared with the lean years of the immediate past, and of challenges that appear at least equally daunting. From their present narrow base as obligatory subjects in Secondary 1 and 2, it has become national policy that foreign languages should expand in a number of directions.

First, and most obviously, they will expand into Secondary 3 and 4 as obligatory subjects for all learners. This means that Scottish pupils will still have one year less of a compulsory foreign language than their counterparts in England and Wales, and fewer still than young people on the continent of Europe. Nevertheless, this welcome change is a major undertaking for national and regional providers of resources, for school managers and for classroom teachers.

Second, at the same time, and increasingly over the years, they will be taught in Primary Schools - "they" being the operative term, because French will not dominate. In the words of Mr Forsyth, offering a foreign language in Primary School will be: "... one of the most exciting new developments that we have in mind." It is at present not clear just how far down the Primary School and how widespread across Primary Schools the development will extend. In principle, it ought to embrace all Primary Schools in the country, otherwise continuity into Secondary education will be compromised. The choice of language offered needs to be made regionally within an agreed national framework. Furthermore, if the real benefits of foreign languages in the Primary School are to be obtained, then desirably they should extend down beyond Primary 7.

Third, languages will gradually be used within other subjects. In Tony Giovanazzi's words: "... the context for language-learning must be drawn more and more from the areas of students' other studies". This indicates that in time foreign languages will begin to escape from their conventional framing as self-contained school "subjects". Indeed, if foreign languages are not used "for real" by learners and others outside the subject classroom, it is very doubtful if the expectations raised by 1992 will be fulfilled.

Fourth, plans will undoubtedly be made for attracting many more students to continue with foreign languages in Secondary 5 and 6 - arguably as important a development as the other three.

It would be naive to expect widespread and highly successful developments on all four fronts. In the short term, priority should no doubt be given to ensuring that all learners in Secondary 1 to 4 should take a successful foreign-language course leading to Standard Grade within a national framework of diversified foreign-language provision.

Whilst it will be important to secure resourcing in order to produce new materials, to refine existing methods and to exploit the potential of the new technologies, the main resource problem for the next few years is undoubtedly one of teacher supply.

The Scottish Education Department has estimated that some 400-500 additional foreign-language teachers will be required in order to implement the Secretary of State's policy statement on foreign languages in 1992. It is now fairly clear that this number will be needed simply to cater for the increased population of foreign-language learners in Secondary 1 to 4; it will not cater for the expansion of foreign languages in Primary Schools and in the later stages of Secondary. Additional teachers will be needed for these two purposes.

In the primary schools, the main bulk of the teaching at the experimental stage is to be carried out by secondary teachers visiting primary schools in the catchment area of their own secondary school. This implies a need for training, both for the secondary teachers and for the staff of the primary schools who will work in collaboration with them. In the longer run, it is doubtful if this arrangement for teaching languages in the primary school represents a desirable or even a feasible model. Primary teachers, themselves, will have to develop the levels of foreign-language competence which will enable them to introduce foreign languages to their pupils. In this connection, it would be naive to assume that a four-year language course at secondary, leading to Standard Grade, or in time even a five-year course consisting of one year at Primary plus four years at Secondary, would adequately equip future cohorts of Primary school teachers for the task of offering a foreign language to their pupils. Much more information on this important issue is needed than appears at present to be available.

At Secondary level, not only will there be a need for a large number of additional foreign-language teachers, but in some cases their level of foreign-ianguage oral competence may need to be extended. If at present not all teachers feel totally at their ease in meeting the oral demands of teaching (say) a Standard Grade course in Secondary 3 and 4, what might their feeling be if, in the future, they are asked to take a Secondary 3 or 4 class that was in its 5th, 6th or even 7th year of learning the foreign language?

Increased staff-mobility post-1992 might conceivably mean that suitably qualified foreign nationals from other EEC countries may come to Scotland in order to teach. This would offer the exciting prospect of using a foreign language to teach other subjects, eg geography and social studies. But will salary levels in this country attract them?

Indeed, what incentive will there be in this country that will attract young native Scots foreign-language graduates to opt for the teaching profession?

Projections for the early to mid-1990's indicate a worrying disharmony of demographic trend and educational need: an overall increase in the number of pupils going through the secondary education, all of whom, as a result of government policy, will be taking a foreign language from Secondary 1 to 4, but at the same time a drop in the number projected to be leaving Higher Education with degrees. In short, a major increase of foreign-language learners in secondary schools, but a drop in the number of potential new teachers. To add to the difficulty, there will be severe competition from other and more lucrative professions for the reduced number of graduates, including (possibly pre-eminently) those with degrees in foreign languages. How attractive will the job of school teaching appear to them in this light?

We accordingly believe that it will not suffice simply to raise the general consciousness of the national need for good-quality foreign-language teachers and then to wait and see how many enrol for particular initial-training courses. If the highly desirable policies on foreign-language teaching, to which the country is now committed, are to attain the success they deserve, then they must be matched by equally determined and explicit policies on teacher supply.

In the words of Professor Forty: "It will require a major effort to provide teachers with the skills to meet this new challenge".

May 1989

GLOSSARY OF EDUCATIONAL TERMS AND ACRONYMS

BOTB   British Overseas Trade Board

CAST   Curriculum and Assessment Support Team

CILT   Centre for Information on Language Teaching and Research

CNAA   Council for National Academic Awards

COMETT   Programme of the European Community in Education and Training for Technology

CSYS   Certificate of Sixth Year Studies

DELTA   European Community project: Developing European learning through Technological Advance

ERASMUS   European Community action scheme for the mobility of university students

LINGUA   European Community language programme that aims: i) to increase the capacity of citizens of the Community to communicate with each other by an improvement in teaching and learning of foreign languages, and ii) to ensure effective measures towards the provision of the necessary levels of foreign-language expertise in the present and future workforce in order to enable enterprises to take full advantage of the Internal Market

NFER   National Foundation for Educational Research: conducted the well-known evaluation of French in the Primary Schools in the late 1960's

SCDI   Scottish Council for Development and Industry

SCOTVEC   Scottish Vocational Education Council

TVEI   Technical Vocational Education Initiative

Items 1 - 8   :   YOUR FIRM AND ITS FOREIGN BUSINESS

Items 9 - 19 :   YOUR FIRM'S CURRENT USE AND NEED
                   OF FOREIGN LANGUAGES

Items 20 - 30 :   THE PROVISION OF FOREIGN-LANGUAGE
                   EXPERTISE TO YOUR FIRM

1. How many people work   *   1-50
    for your firm in Scotland?   *   51-200
                                   *   201-500
                                   *   500+

2. What way you approximate
    turnover last year?   £ ....

    Or

    If you are a financial
    institution, what was the
    size of your balance-sheet?   £ ....

3. At present, approximately   Areas/Countries
    what percentage of your
    exports / overseas   French-speaking   .....%
    earnings does each of   German-speaking   .....%
    the following areas /   Spanish-speaking   .....%
    countries account for?   Arabic-speaking   .....%
                                  Italy   .....%
                                  USSR   .....%
                                  Japan   .....%
                                  ....%
                                  ....%

4. Over the next 1-5 years do you expect the earnings indicated in 3. above to grow, stay the same or diminish?

They are likely to grow
in these areas

* French-speaking
* German-speaking
* Spanish-speaking
* Arabic-speaking
* Italy
* USSR
* Japan
* ....
* ....

They are likely to stay
the same in these areas

* French-speaking
* German-speaking
* Spanish speaking
* Arabic-speaking
* Italy
* USSR
* ....
* ....

They are likely to
diminish in these areas

* French-speaking
* German-speaking
* Spanish speaking
* Arabic-speaking
* Italy
* USSR
* Japan
* ....
* ....

5. Does your firm subscribe
to any foreign-language
trade journals?

* French   * Italian
* German   * Russian
* Spanish   * Japanese
* Arabic   * ....
* ....

6. Within the last three years
has your firm produced any
promotional material in a
foreign language?

* French   * Italian
* German   * Russian
* Spanish   * Japanese
* Arabic   * ....
* ....

7. Within the last three years   * French-speaking
    has your firm employed an   * German-speaking
    agent or distributor in any   * Spanish speaking
    foreign-language speaking   * Arabic-speaking
    country/area   * Italy
                                    * USSR
                                    * Japan
                                    * ....
                                    * ....

8. Does you firm have any   * French-speaking
    associate companies in   * German-speaking
    foreign-language speaking   * Spanish speaking
    countries/areas   * Arabic-speaking
    (eg subsidiary or parent   * Italy
    company, legal or accounting   * USSR
    firm)?   * Japan
                                    * ....
                                    * ....

9. At present, when a letter, fax or telex written in a foreign language is
    received by your firm, what happens to it?

    It is read and actioned   * French   * Italian
    by the Managing Director   * German   * Russian
                                 * Spanish   * Japanese
                                 * Arabic   * ....
                                 * ....

    It is translated by   * French   * Italian
    another member of staff   * German   * Russian
                                 * Spanish   * Japanese
                                 * Arabic   * ....
                                 * ....

    It is sent to an external   * French   * Italian
    agency for translation   * German   * Russian
                                 * Spanish   * Japanese
                                 * Arabic   * ....
                                 * ....

    It is not read   * French   * Italian
                                 * German   * Russian
                                 * Spanish   * Japanese
                                 * Arabic   * ....
                                 * ....

    Other (please specify)

10. On average, how long does it take before the contents of a foreign-language letter, fax or telex become available to be actioned?

It is dealt with
immediately

* French   * Italian
* German   * Russian
* Spanish   * Japanese
* Arabic   * ....
* ....

It takes less than
24 hours

* French   * Italian
* German   * Russian
* Spanish   * Japanese
* Arabic   * ....
* ....

It takes 2 to 3
days

* French   * Italian
* German   * Russian
* Spanish   * Japanese
* Arabic   * ....
* ....

It takes a week
or more

* French   * Italian
* German   * Russian
* Spanish   * Japanese
* Arabic   * ....
* ....

11. When your firm replies
to a letter written in
a foreign language, what
language do you use?

* French   or * English
* German   or * English
* Spanish   or * English
* Italian   or * English
* Russian   or * English
* Japanese or * English
* ....   or * English
* ....   or * English

12. At present, in your translations with areas/countries in which English is not a first language, what languages do you use?

We mainly/entirely
use English

* French-speaking
* German-speaking
* Spanish speaking
* Arabic-speaking
* Italy
* USSR
* Japan
* ....
* ....

We regularly use both
English and the foreign
language, in roughly
equal measure

* French-speaking
* German-speaking
* Spanish speaking
* Arabic-speaking
* Italy
* USSR
* Japan
* ....
* ....

We mainly/entirely use
the foreign language

* French-speaking
* German-speaking
* Spanish speaking
* Arabic-speaking
* Italy
* USSR
* Japan
* ....
* ....

13. Over the next 1-5 years do you envisage that your firm's need for foreign languages will grow, stay the same or diminish?

Our need is likely to grow	* French	* Italian
	* German	* Russian
	* Spanish	* Japanese
	* Arabic	* ....
	*	

Our need is likely to stay the same	* French	* Italian
	* German	* Russian
	* Spanish	* Japanese
	* Arabic	* ....
	*	

Our need is likely to diminish	* French	* Italian
	* German	* Russian
	* Spanish	* Japanese
	* Arabic	* ....
	*	

14. What are the main activities for which your firm has used a foreign language in trade contacts with other countries?

* Entertaining & socialising
* Using the phone
* Discussion, eg in buying/ selling/negotiating
* Reading letters, telex, fax
* Reading technical/sales texts
* Listening to talks
* Giving talks & speeches
* Writing letters
* Writing trade documents
* Writing technical manuals
* Drafting legal agreements
* ....
* ....

                                 More   Same   Less

15 Over the next   *   *   *   Entertaining & socialising
    1-5 years, do you   *   *   *   Using the Phone
    envisage that your   *   *   *   Travelling abroad
    need of any of these   *   *   *   Discussion, eg in buying,
    foreign-language   *   *   *   selling, negotiating
    activities is likely   *   *   *   Reading letters, telex, fax
    grow, stay the same   *   *   *   Reading technical/sales
    or diminish?   *   *   *   texts
                               *   *   *   Listening to talks
    If grow, ring More   *   *   *   Giving talks, speeches
    If same, ring Same   *   *   *   Writing letters
    If diminish, ring Less   *   *   *   Writing trade documents
                               *   *   *   Writing technical manuals
                               *   *   *   Drafting legal agreements
                               *   *   *   ....
                               *   *   *   ....

16. Which categories of your   *   Managerial/Executive
    personnel currently use   *   Secretarial/Receptionist
    foreign languages for   *   Advertising/Marketing
    purposes related to their *   Sales
    job?   *   Production
                               *   Research
                               *   Accounts
                               *   Design
                               *   Purchasing
                               *   Contracts
                               *   Finance
                               *   Transport/Distribution
                               *   ....
                               *   ....

More Same Less

17. Within each cate-   *   *   *   Managerial/Executive
    gory of personnel   *   *   *   Secretarial/Receptionist
    do you envisage   *   *   *   Advertising/Marketing
    that the need for   *   *   *   Sales
    a foreign-language   *   *   *   Production
    will grow, stay the   *   *   *   Research
    same or diminish   *   *   *   Accounts
    over the next 1-5   *   *   *   Design
    years?   *   *   *   Purchasing
                                *   *   *   Contracts
    If grow, ring More   *   *   *   Finance
    If same, ring Same   *   *   *   Transport/Distribution
    If diminish, ring Less   *   *   *   ....

18. Do you believe there are   If Yes, please ring
    any areas/countries for   the foreign-languages
    which a better command of
    a foreign language could   * French * Italian
    significantly benefit   * German * Russian
    your firm?   * Spanish * Japanese
                                     * Arabic * ....
                                     * ....

19. Do you believe there are   If Yes, please ring
    any areas/countries for   the areas/countries
    which a greater knowledge
    of social and business   *   French-speaking
    protocol and practice   *   German-speaking
    could significantly   *   Spanish speaking
    benefit your firm?   *   Arabic-speaking
                                     *   Italy
                                     *   USSR
                                     *   Japan
                                     *   ....
                                     *   ....

20. Within the last three years have you taken on to your staff, either permanently or temporarily, any Modern Languages graduates?

*   Yes   *   No

If Yes, what benefits have they brought to your firm?

*   Command of a foreign language
*   Knowledge of customs, attitudes ways of life in foreign country
*   General ability to communicate in speech and in writing
*   Ability to analyse situations
*   ....
*   ....

21. Within the last five years, have you used the command of a foreign language as one criterion when you set out to recruit a new members of staff?

*   Yes *   No

If No, proceed to Item 24

22. If you answered Yes to Item 21, what category or categories of staff were you looking for?

*   Managerial/Executive
*   Secretarial/Receptionist
*   Advertising/Marketing
*   Sales
*   Production
*   Research
*   Accounts
*   Design
*   Purchasing
*   Contracts
*   Finance
*   Transport/Distribution
*   ....

23. If you answered Yes to Item 21, what language or languages did you wish the new recruit(s) to be able to use?

How successful were you in finding applicants with the required foreign-languages skills?

* French   * successful
           * unsuccessful

* German   * successful
           * unsuccessful

* Spanish * successful
           * unsuccessful

* Arabic   * successful
           * unsuccessful

* Italian * successful
           * unsuccessful

* Russian * successful
           * unsuccessful

* Japanese * successful
           * unsuccessful

* .... * successful
             * unsuccessful

* .... * successful
             * unsuccessful

24. From the point of view of your firm, how satisfied are you that the educational system (eg schools, colleges, universities) is producing the right people with the right skills to meet your foreign-languages needs?

* Very satisfied
* Fairly satisfied
* Partly satisfied
* Not satisfied
* Not at all satisfied

If you answered Very or Fairly, proceed to Item 26

25. If in Item 24 you   *   A wider range of foreign
    answered Partly, Not   languages
    or Not at all, what
    more is required to   *   More graduate linguists
    meet the needs of your
    firm?   *   More graduates in business and
                                  management with competence in a
                                  foreign-language

                            *   More trained professional, research,
                                  technical, scientific staff with
                                  competence in a foreign-language

                            *   More secretarial staff with competence
                                  in a foreign-language

                            *   Greater emphasis on technical and
                                  commercial language in foreign-
                                  language courses

                            *   Greater integration of foreign language
                                  teaching with commercial and technical
                                  teaching

                            *   ....

26. Over the last three years,   * Yes   * No
    has your firm used the
    services of a translating   If Yes, how satisfied were
    -interpreting agency?   were you with the service
    provided?

                                   *   Very satisfied
                                   *   Fairly satisfied
                                   *   Partly satisfied
                                   *   Not satisfied
                                   *   Not at all satisfied

    If you answered Very or Fairly, proceed to Item 28

27. If in Item 26, you answered   *   Greater accuracy
     Partly, Not or Not at all,   *   Faster service
     what more is required to   *   More local service
     help meet the needs of your   *   Wider range of languages
     firm?   *   ....

28. Over the last three years,   *   Yes   *   No
     has your firm used the
     services of a language   If Yes, how satisfied were
     school?   you with the service provided?

                                     *   Very satisfied
                                     *   Fairly satisfied
                                     *   Partly satisfied
                                     *   Not satisfied
                                     *   Not at all satisfied

     If you answered Very or Fairly, proceed to Item 30

29. If in Item 28 you answered   *   Faster service
     Partly, Not or Not at all,   *   Wider range of languages
     what more is required to   *   More flexible delivery of
     meet your needs?   courses
                                     *   Specialised course
                                     *   Intensive courses
                                     *   ....

30. If in view of the Single   *   Yes   *   No
     European Act of 1992, does
     your firm have, or does it
     intend to adopt, a policy
     of encouraging staff to
     improve and make use of
     their knowledge of
     foreign-languages?

     If Yes, could you briefly describe this policy in the space below?